M

C000286012

Mary
Wollstonecraft
Shelley

An Introduction

~

Betty T. Bennett

The Johns Hopkins
University Press
Baltimore & London

© Pickering and Chatto (Publishers) Limited 1996
New material ©1998 The Johns Hopkins University Press
All rights reserved. Published 1998
Printed in the United States of America on acid-free paper

9 8 7 6 5 4 3 2 1

The Johns Hopkins University Press
2715 North Charles Street
Baltimore, Maryland 21218-4363
The Johns Hopkins Press Ltd., London

This volume is a revision and expansion of the introduction
to *The Novels and Selected Works of Mary Shelley,* published in 1996
by Pickering and Chatto.

Title-page portrait: Mary Wollstonecraft Shelley, a miniature by
Reginald Easton, courtesy of the Bodleian Library.

Library of Congress Cataloging-in-Publication Data will be
found at the end of this book.
A catalog record for this book is available from the British
Library.

ISBN 0-8018-5975-1
ISBN 0-8018-5976-X (pbk.)

What should I have done if
Alice G. Fredman, Stuart Curran,
and Charles E. Robinson
had not been my Mary Shelley
companions?

Contents

Preface

For many years, Mary Wollstonecraft Shelley has been generally represented as a one-book author. Since that book is *Frankenstein,* the single best known work of the Romantic era, it might seem sufficient. But there is far more to Mary Shelley. There are five other novels, a novella, two travel books, two mythical dramas, five volumes of biographical lives, short stories, essays, poems, and her monumental editions of the works of her husband, Percy Bysshe Shelley. There are the complexities of a precocious girl and an astute woman; of a person who, by birth and by calling, chose to become an author; and of an author who developed a unique voice in literary history.

But as easy as it is to find a copy of *Frankenstein* in libraries and bookstores worldwide, finding copies of Mary Shelley's other works has been a challenge if not an impossibility. In recent decades, editions of *The Last Man* have become more available, and several other novels were reprinted in exceedingly limited and expensive editions. For the most part, however, her other works have remained accessible only on the shelves of rare book rooms and private collectors. Without these works, general readers and scholars alike have been deprived of the means to recognize the complexities of Mary Shelley's imagination and how she used that imagination to portray the social and political systems of nineteenth-century European society.

The publisher Pickering and Chatto, realizing this deficiency, proposed an eight-volume edition that would, for the first time, collect Mary Shelley's novels and selected other works. Their invitation to me to assemble a team of scholars to produce this edition also provided the occasion to write an overall introduction that would tie the volumes to each other and to Mary Shelley's life. *The Novels and Selected Works of Mary Shelley* was published in 1996, a fitting prelude to the 1997 worldwide celebrations of the bicentennial of the author's birth.

The process of editing *The Letters of Mary Wollstonecraft Shelley* brought forward a Mary Shelley quite different from the Victorianized, dependent figure depicted in nineteenth- and most twentieth-century studies. The letters revealed that, from the close of the Napoleanic Wars through the growth of the industrial and mercantile wars, from the idealism of the French Revolution to the slow accretion of democracy in Britain, Mary Shelley observed, commented, and criticized. She perceptively linked personal politics with public politics and advocated that both spheres replace traditional power-based sociopolitical systems with the humanistic alternative of universal love. More than any other Romantic author, she was directly experienced in the revolutionary changes in the world around her which forged the beginnings of modern society. All of this she inscribed in her writing. The work of the Introduction to the *Novels and Selected Works* was to allow Mary Shelley's own focus: to represent her as a political, cosmopolitan author whose astute perceptions and artistic expression spanned some three decades.

Shortly after the appearance of the Pickering and Chatto edition, the Johns Hopkins University Press indicated its interest in republishing the introduction as a monograph. I have taken this opportunity to rethink, revise, and considerably expand the earlier version. The work here is still an introduction. It is not meant to be comprehensive in scope, but it is meant to provide a way of seeing and understanding Mary Shelley as I believe she saw herself— an inventive, irreverent writer who fostered an agenda of democratic, political, and social reform. In 1817, she wrote in a letter, "You see what a John or rather Joan Bull I am so full politics" (*MWSL*, I, 139); in 1830, "Will not our Children live to see a new birth to the world!" (*MWSL*, II, 168); in 1848, "We boast of our improved lights—& our books overflow with philosophical principles, yet our public men perpetually make the grossest mistakes, & all they do, had better be left undone" (*MWSL*, III, 341). In her novels and other professional writing, Mary Shelley expressed her reformist philosophy in unusual configurations through which readers are invited—if we dare—to explore not only her imagination but our own.

Many colleagues and friends have contributed to the revised introduction in different and significant ways. I am deeply indebted to Lord Abinger, the Carl H. Pforzheimer Library, and the Bodleian Library, all of whom have generously permitted me to study and publish from their collections over many years. Special thanks are also due to the team of scholars who produced the *Novels and Selected Works* for modern readers, most notably Nora Crook, for her distinguished editorial work.

I wish also to thank a number of colleagues at American University. Jonathan Loesberg and Richard Sha of the Literature Department read the revised manuscript of the revised introduction and posed insightful questions; Jonathan reread the next version, as well, a deed generous in scholarship and friendship. In various and supportive ways, the following also aided this edition: Alexandra Boose, Tisha Brady, and Mary Mintz, as well as the College of Arts and Sciences and, especially, Kathleen Kennedy-Corey.

Many other friends, over a long period of time, have also generously shared their scholarship with me. Special thanks go to: Stuart Curran, the late Alice G. Fredman, Christina M. Gee, Hilton Kelliher, Edward Kessler, Donald H. Reiman, Charles E. Robinson, William St Clair, and Marion K. Stocking.

It is a pleasure to acknowledge Douglas Armato, Joanne Allen, and Barbara Lamb at the Johns Hopkins University Press for their enthusiastic support of this edition.

Over these years, my family, so giving in love and encouragement, has changed its form and boundaries. But I count as Wordsworth's child in "We Are Seven" counted and, with enduring love, thank them all.

Mary Wollstonecraft Shelley

CHAPTER ONE

Early Journeys, 1797–1818

ARY Wollstonecraft Shelley was born on 30 August 1797. Her father, the philosopher and novelist William Godwin (1756–1836), recorded the moment in his daily journal: "Birth of Mary, 20 minutes after 11 at night." Eleven days later, her mother, the philosopher and novelist Mary Wollstonecraft Godwin (b. 1759), died of puerperal fever, and Godwin entered the simple note: "20 minutes before 8."[1]

Mary Shelley, then, from the moment of her birth, was linked to her parents not only genetically but also through the written word. That written legacy included Mary Wollstonecraft's *A Vindication of the Rights of Woman with Strictures on Political and Moral Subjects* (1792) and *Letters Written during a Short Residence in Sweden, Norway, and Denmark* (1796).[2] The first endures as a pioneering argument espousing, for the benefit of the individual and the society as a whole, equal education and equal status for women. The second illustrates the value of such education and status through the author's transformation of personal letters into a proto-Romantic journey of mind and spirit. Godwin, whose dissenting heritage marginalized him from the outset, had already produced the two works that would stand as his master-pieces: *An Enquiry Concerning Political Justice* (1793), his anti-monarchical argument for a republican, and minimal, form of government, and *Caleb Williams* (1794), a fictional attack on the same social values that *Political Justice* critiqued in its call for radical reform.[3] Wollstonecraft and Godwin gave voice to the revolutionary impulses of their day; influencing like-minded thinkers, they were rejected by adherents to the status quo. Remarkably, one of their most illustrious disciples would prove to be their own daughter.

Mary Shelley modeled her life and works on her parents' belief in the power and responsibility of the individual to effect change, on their own activist and risk-taking engagement with their society, and on their ability to recognize transition—in themselves and in the society—and to respond accordingly. Her masterpiece *Frankenstein,* the five novels that followed, her travel books, biographical lives, essays, as well as her editions of Percy Bysshe Shelley's works, consistently demonstrate this dual political and literary influence.

But just as Mary Shelley grew up in a milieu that formed her own unusual experience of social class, family structure, and historical context, she developed a reformist sociopolitical vision particular to those experiences through which she challenged the conservative politics, civic and personal, that flourished in her own lifetime. It is a singular fact of literary history that her central political vision grapples with the very social, scientific, industrial, and economic issues that, emerging in her era, continue to trouble modern society to this day. Mary Shelley's contemporary reviewers, however, considered politics a male topic and thus failed to evaluate her novels with this key in mind. In our era, much important work has been accomplished in resituating women's writing historically. But with few exceptions,[4] the vast majority of literary critics read the works of women as apolitical or principally concerned with the female and domestic spheres as separate from the public sphere.[5] As a result, Mary Shelley's works mostly remain subsumed within generalized theories of women's writing rather than being considered on their own, independent terms.

Mary Shelley, however, resisted the segregation of the public and private and its hierarchical division of power and responsibility. To the contrary, she believed that the sociopolitical iniquities of the larger society were mirrored within the family and the individual. She delineates this thesis by invariably coalescing the private and the public. All of the principal figures in her novels, and many of the minor ones, exemplify this correlation, their particular struggles never apart from the societal influence that engendered them.

Recognition of Mary Shelley's systemic dual focus on public *and* domestic power as the means to interrogate traditional norms and propose alternatives materially alters parochial perceptions of her objectives and her achievements. Her novels, outside of *Frankenstein* and, recently, *The Last Man,* have been dismissed as simple, mutually dissociated "romances" or experiments in genre solely to intersect with a market niche; they are neither. Rather, they and all of Mary Shelley's major works voice a cosmopolitan, sociopolitical reformist ideology that evolved as their author's acute awareness of world events enabled her to calibrate her literary voice to deal with unfolding rather than past societal issues. Her multidisciplinary fusion of literature, political philosophy, and history calls for a commensurate multidisciplinary reading in order to understand the complexities of both the author and her works.

Only two decades separated her birth and her parents' radical writings from Mary Shelley's first published book. But the war between Britain and France, 1793–1815, which encompassed the first seventeen years of Mary Shelley's life, was a period in which the political and literary reformist voices of her parents' generation were gradually silenced through governmental pressure and conservative oppression. Godwin and Wollstonecraft, and the other reformers in the closing decade of the eighteenth century, had envisioned the French Revolution as an opportunity to reorder a world that had, with their approval, fragmented. Most reformers believed this fragmentation to be a temporary condition, antecedent to an enlightened, democratized world they would help create. A fundamental difference, however, existed among the reformers themselves. Godwin, along with other Enlightenment adherents, endorsed an outcome that would introduce into society an ongoing, evolutionary process based on universal education with an attainable goal of human perfectibility.[6] Other reformers, including the first generation of Romantic poets—with Wordsworth, Coleridge, and Southey at the forefront—imagined a new world with new values but one that would replicate the old order in being stable and holistic.

The conclusion of the Napoleonic Wars instead brought unemployment, inflation, and sociopolitical upheaval, the very antithesis of the dreams of the early 1790s. At the same time, despite efforts by machine-breaking Luddites, another destabilizing but more proficient revolution occurred: the industrial revolution. By the second decade of the nineteenth century the dominance of three hundred years of agrarian society had ended, and the population, willingly or not, flooded into the expanding cities that were to become the centers of industry and commerce.[7]

The older Romantics, through the metaphors of nature and religion, still struggled to reclaim order from the instability of almost twenty-five years of war and its aftermath. In contrast, Mary Shelley and P. B. Shelley (1792–1822) both projected a new world order based on an assumption of continuous process rather than stasis. In this they reflected Godwin and Wollstonecraft's belief in an attainable democratic society structured on reason and social progress, inculcated through universal education.[8] But Mary Shelley, by inclination and influenced by P. B. Shelley, altered the emphasis on reason in favor of a philosophy that advocated universal love as well.[9] The Shelleys, perhaps in reaction to the disappointments of reformers of the previous generation, projected this newly configured nucleus as the genesis of a cyclical but nevertheless ever-advancing social system established on democratic ideals of justice. Mary Shelley's distinctive application of these principles transfigured her works from simply the echo of her parents' and her husband's works into a fully evolved Romantic voice of her own.

That voice reflects an upbringing that instilled confidence in her own agency to influence and effect change. Unlike her parents' works, written in an era of revolutionary expectation, her works promote egalitarian values in a quickly entrenching Victorian society constructed on a narrow, rigid, and self-serving mercantilism. Both Shelleys recognized this major historical shift. But P. B. Shelley, privileged by family wealth as well as gender, generally addressed his works to a like audience. In contrast, Mary Shelley's family and gender gave her firsthand experience of life as a marginalized member of society. She expressed that experience in her novels in a blend of resolute candor about individual human foibles and an empathy demonstrating that such flaws are a result of the social condition and therefore correctable through individual and societal self-restructure. Her novels also depict humanistic idealism and valor on the part of women and men, but often where least expected in terms of gender and background.

Mary Shelley wrote and published relatively few formally structured poems; some seventeen have been identified to date.[10] About these she commented, "I can never write verses except under the influence of a strong sentiment & seldom even then."[11] Her poems appear to reflect that inspiration. Written in the first person, they are Romantically confessional and mostly dwell on death, the loss of love, and solitude. But Mary Shelley expresses another, less traditional form of poetry through the meditative impulse she inventively weaves throughout her longer prose. In these interposed poetic intervals the narrative voice invites readers to consider, for themselves and for the characters in the novels, the repercussions as individual responses vie with societal indoctrination. Frequently the poetry in the novels also tacitly exemplifies Mary Shelley's belief in the potential beauty, love, and humanism that endure in life despite its dilemmas.

Her parents' sociopsychological fiction, written to reach an audience that would not be attracted to political tract, clearly influenced their daughter's own literary technique. Mary Shelley wrote fiction to reach those same strata of society. In her time that audience was far larger and, though more privileged and gradually achieving some of the benefits of democracy, perhaps more limited by its failure of humanistic imagination.

Mary Shelley's voice developed early, influenced by her unconventional childhood, in which politics, writing, and family were freely associated. To begin with, at Wollstonecraft's death Godwin, a forty-year-old bachelor when he married, was left with not one but two daughters. Godwin informally adopted Fanny Godwin (1794–1816), Mary Wollstonecraft's natural child by Gilbert Imlay, as his daughter and gave her his name.[12] Faced with the challenge of caring for the two children, Godwin had yet a larger challenge that would greatly affect Mary Shelley's life. Godwin had developed his own theories of education.[13] He employed them first with a private pupil and then with the twelve-year-old Thomas Abthorpe Cooper, who lived in Godwin's household from 1788 to 1792.[14] And Mary Wollstonecraft left a significant legacy of works about raising daughters, including *Thoughts on the Education of Daughters; The Female Reader . . . for the Improvement of Young Women;* and the *Vindication.*[15] Aided by nursemaids and governesses, supplemented by relatives and friends, Godwin might have been able to meet the demands of rearing his daughters, on whom he doted.[16] Neither he nor they, however, could supply the presence of his beloved companion. The depth of his love for Wollstonecraft inspired him to modify his philosophic theories in the second and third editions of *Political Justice* to add "private affections" to his abiding confidence in reason as the basis for societal conduct.[17] After several abortive courtships,[18] in 1801 Godwin met and married Mary Jane (Vial) Clairmont (1768–1841), who brought with her two natural children, Charles Gaulis Clairmont (1795–1850) and Clara Mary Jane (Claire) Clairmont (1798–1879).

The illegitimacy of these children and Fanny Godwin, perhaps objectionable to another middle-class family of the era, did not perturb the philosopher Godwin. He and Wollstonecraft both opposed legal marriage on the grounds that it made servants of women and constrained couples to remain united by law rather than by choice. In an ideal world the law would have no authority over personal relationships. However, they recognized that contemporary society, legally and often socially, disenfranchised illegitimate children and their mothers. In protection, unmarried middle-class women often styled themselves "Mrs.," as Mary Wollstonecraft had in calling herself "Mrs. Imlay." Godwin and Wollstonecraft, to safeguard their expected child, married in March 1797, just five months before Mary Shelley's birth. It is likely that Godwin and Clairmont's marriage in December 1801 was also prompted by her pregnancy, which miscarried.[19] In 1803 the couple had William Godwin Jr., bringing the family configuration to the father-philosopher-writer-stepfather, the mother-writer-stepmother, five children, and the ever-present shade of Mary Wollstonecraft Godwin. In her early years Mary Shelley coped with an "excessive & romantic attachment" to her father[20] and an antipathetic relationship with her stepmother, and four siblings, who ranged from three years older to six years younger than she and who were, and were not, her brothers and sisters. In this household she had an uncommon education in power and intellect, love and solitude.

By circumstance all of the Godwins had to negotiate their lives within their large, assorted family, which both parents constantly struggled to support. Godwin, his study lined with hundreds of books and presided over by John Opie's portrait of Mary Wollstonecraft, set a lofty intellectual standard for everyone in the household.[21] Years later, Claire Clairmont complained that in the Godwin home, "if you cannot write an epic poem or a novel that by its originality knocks all other novels on the head, you are a despicable creature not worth acknowledging."[22]

The intellectual expectations of Mary Shelley's heritage and her own precocity set her apart from the other children in the family. When she was three weeks old, she was the subject of a physiognomic assessment—closely linked to the then popular theory of phrenology—by Godwin's close friend, the scientist William Nicholson.[23] Nicholson conjectured that she possessed "considerable intelligence and memory."[24] Godwin was assessed by a phrenologist in 1820. Though he later rejected the tenets of phrenology in his 1831 *Thoughts on Man* essay,[25] his confidence in his daughter's abilities never wavered.

Mary Shelley voiced her own recognition of that expectation in the 1831 introduction to *Frankenstein:* "It is not singular that, as the daughter of two persons of distinguished literary celebrity, I should very early in life have thought of writing. As a child I scribbled; and my favorite pastime, during the hours given me for recreation, was to `write stories.' Still I had a dearer pleasure than this . . . the in-

dulging in waking dreams—the following up trains of
thought, which had for their subject the formation of a
succession of imaginary incidents" (*N&SW*, 1:175).[26]

Mary Shelley's cultivation in the world of books was extended to include an early apprenticeship in publishing
and bookselling. Financially hard-pressed, the Godwins in
1805 established a publishing firm–bookselling shop ded-
icated to children's books, a lucrative enterprise of the period.[27] In 1807 they relocated the shop on the ground
floor of 41 Skinner Street and the family to the apartment
above. The company was named M. J. Godwin & Company, dissociating the enterprise from Godwin, who since
the end of the 1790s had kept a relatively low public profile
because his politics were in strong disfavor. Acknowledging
that his serious writing was insufficient to meet the family's
financial needs, Godwin wrote a number of highly successful works for children under the pseudonyms Theophilus
Marcliffe and Edward Baldwin.[28] In 1808 the young Mary
Shelley was called on by Godwin to contribute a draft to the
writing of the satire *Mounseer Nongtongpaw,* published by the
family company (*N&SW*, 8:397–406).

The conservatism in British public feeling affected Godwin's life and consequently his daughter's, not only politically but personally. Almost immediately after Mary Wollstonecraft's death, Godwin, in his deep grief, turned to the
written word, the medium he and Wollstonecraft had so
singularly shared. He undertook two projects to celebrate
more the author and the individual than the wife, editing

her manuscripts for *Posthumous Works of the Author of a Vindication of the Rights of Woman* and at the same time writing an extraordinarily frank recounting of her life, including her love relationships, in *Memoirs of the Author of a Vindication of the Rights of Woman.*[29] The *Memoirs* gave the conservative press the occasion to scathingly attack both author and subject. Godwin, who sought to memorialize Wollstonecraft, found the volumes denounced as "shameless," "lascivious" and "disgusting" and their subject, because of the illegitimate Fanny Godwin, labeled a "prostitute" in vitriolic attacks that clouded her name well into the century.[30] Mary Shelley's special affinity for those who admired her mother—"The memory of my Mother has been always been [*sic*] the pride & delight of my life; & the admiration of others for her, has been the cause of most of the happiness «of my life» I have enjoyed"[31]—suggests that she was aware of her mother's disrepute, though from what age is unclear.[32]

The attacks on the *Memoirs* may have influenced Godwin's response to a query about whether his daughter was being educated according to her mother's precepts. He replied that "the present Mrs. Godwin has great strength and activity of mind, but is not exclusively a follower of the notions" of Wollstonecraft and that both of them, pressed by the need to support the family, had not "leisure enough for reducing novel theories of education to practice, while we both of us honestly endeavor, as far as our opportunities will permit, to improve the mind and characters of the younger branches of our family."[33] Despite this disclaimer, however, Mary Shelley's education did reflect the most significant aspect of her mother's radical theories of education for women: "[T]he most perfect education, in my opinion, is such an exercise of the understanding as is best calculated to strengthen the body and form the heart. . . . to enable the individual to attain such habits of virtue as will render it independent. . . . through the exercise of its own reason."[34]

It is uncertain which of her mother's writings she read before 1814, but it is quite apparent that Godwin and his friends revered Wollstonecraft and that Mary Shelley fully embraced those feelings. It was her habit to go to St. Pancras Churchyard and read by her mother's four-sided "sacred tomb," both place and books precious connections to her mother.[35] Later it would be the site where "first love shone" in P. B. Shelley's "dear eyes" for her,[36] and until the last years of her life she included "Wollstonecraft," her middle name, or "W," in her signature. It is more than likely that the precocious Mary Shelley had, in her early years, read a number of her mother's works and that Godwin, in his pride, would have willingly provided them to the daughter he described as "singularly bold, somewhat imperious, and active of mind. Her desire of knowledge is great and her perseverance in everything she undertakes, almost invincible."[37]

Godwin's own theories of children's education were at least as radical as Wollstonecraft's. Premised on the necessity of the independent maturation of the imagination,

Godwin's books written for children, including *Bible Stories* (1802), *Fables, Ancient and Modern* (1805), *The History of England* (1806), the *Pantheon: or Ancient History of the Gods of Greece and Rome* (1806), and *History of Rome* (1809), tried out on his own children, were primers for a radical education.[38] Though derived from history and tradition, they were intended to assist young readers in cultivating and trusting their own imaginations—in taking the first steps toward thinking for themselves.[39]

Mary Shelley's education reflected some of the era's traditional subjects for females—reading, writing, French, drawing—but went beyond them in important ways, including, for instance, the study of Latin. Except for netting,[40] Mary Shelley avoided domestic chores when she could,[41] creating a private existence for herself instead in the books that would "people her own world," provide her lifelong company, and, ironically, underscore her sense of exile in her own society.[42]

From 17 May to 19 December 1811 Mary Shelley attended Miss Caroline Petman's school at Ramsgate in the hope that extensive sea-bathing would cure her severely infected arm.[43] How much time she actually attended classes remains unclear, but certainly Miss Petman's was selected because it was a school for the daughters of dissenters. It has been suggested that an unspoken secondary reason for sending her away was to relieve the tension between her and Mrs. Godwin.[44] Mary Shelley's letters attest to that prevalent tension, which apparently was lifelong. Perhaps their

variance stemmed from the girl's overattachment to Godwin and Mary Jane Godwin's partiality towards her own
daughter. Another source surely arose from the second
Mrs. Godwin's knowledge that she was always being unfa-
vorably compared by the Godwin circle with the first Mrs.
Godwin.[45] But also, Mary Shelley's and Mary Jane Godwin's fundamental temperaments differed greatly. For example, Mary Jane Godwin was known to readily lie, "having
no high regard herself for literal truth,"[46] to the irritation
of Godwin and their friends, whereas Mary Shelley followed Godwin's own emphasis on telling the truth. Whatever their differences, however, family values of mutual
responsibility and an ideal of potential improvement prevailed. After Godwin's death and to the end of Mary Jane
Godwin's life, Mary Shelley contributed to her support and
well-being.

Mary Jane Godwin and young William accompanied
Mary Shelley to Ramsgate, just as they had accompanied
Claire Clairmont when she went to Miss Petman's from 3
August to 19 November 1808.[47] Each of the children, most
likely on the basis of available funds rather than because of
family discord, was sent for schooling during various pe-
riods. Fanny Godwin began attending a local day school
shortly before she was five. Two years later, when Mary
Shelley was almost four, she was sent to the same school.[48]
In preparation for careers, both Charles Clairmont and
William Godwin Jr. were sent for formal schooling,[49] and
Claire Clairmont attended a boarding school over a period

of sixteen months to learn French.[50] Perhaps Mary Shelley's experience at Miss Petman's convinced Godwin that his gifted daughter had already surpassed the limited education girls' schools offered, because she received no further formal schooling.

But Mary Shelley had four other sources of education: first, her father's extensive library, which included his books as well as a number of her mother's; second, the Godwins' active education of their children, which included adult lectures, theater, and other events in London to which the children were taken by their parents; third, the stream of extraordinary visitors who frequented the Godwin household, including Samuel Taylor Coleridge, Aaron Burr, Charles and Mary Lamb, who brought to the home a world of ideas and a level of discourse that few girls or boys would have experienced. Nor were the children shunted aside. On the contrary, the children remained in the company of the adults and even performed for guests. For instance, Aaron Burr noted his attendance at a "weekly lecture" entitled "The Influence of governments on the character of a people" in 1812 given by the young William Godwin and written, he believed, by Mary Shelley.[51]

The fourth source of Mary Shelley's education was travel away from home. She remained alone at Miss Petman's (as had Claire Clairmont) after the first month; and on 7 June 1812 her family sent Mary Shelley, in what would be a kind of exchange program, to live with the William Baxter family in Dundee.[52] The Baxters, as well as the lexicographer

David Booth, the husband first of Margaret Baxter and
then of Isabella Baxter, who became Mary Shelley's beloved
friend, were Glassite Calvinists. Their religion was strict,
but their way of life was not. During her stay with the Baxters, Mary Shelley would travel in Scotland, be introduced
to Scottish traditions and myths,[53] and, as she reported in
the 1831 introduction to *Frankenstein,* be relatively free to
write her stories. She remained in Dundee until 10 November 1812, when she returned to London accompanied
by Christy Baxter, another Baxter daughter. The next day
fifteen-year-old Mary Shelley most likely met Godwin and
Wollstonecraft's admirer, the radical poet-philosopher
P. B. Shelley, and his wife Harriet Shelley (1795–1816).
On 3 June 1813 the two young women returned to Dundee, where Mary Shelley remained until she rejoined her
family in Skinner Street on 30 March 1814, having experienced a kind of extended apprenticeship in writing,
travel, and independent thinking.

That May, Mary Shelley and P. B. Shelley again met.
P. B. Shelley, self-estranged from his wife, fell in love
with Godwin and Wollstonecraft's "Child of love and
light."[54] Mary Shelley, echoing Godwin's description of her
as "bold," characterized that period of her life as "careless,
fearless youth."[55] In the same vein, P. B. Shelley praised
her for "[t]he irresi[s]tible wildness & sublimity of her
feelings."[56] For Mary Shelley, the young poet personified
her parents' ardent 1790s reformist ideals.

But Godwin's ardent ideals were situated within the concept of societal evolution. He believed that in an unevolved state individuals had to compromise their ideals to safeguard themselves and their families.[57] Furthermore, the memory of the painful scandal that had erupted years earlier over the Wollstonecraft *Memoirs* and its appropriation by the anti-Jacobin press as a tool to publicly denigrate Wollstonecraft and Godwin both professionally and personally still haunted Godwin. This, as well as other aspects of Godwin's moral code, prompted him to vigorous efforts to prevent the Shelleys' relationship.

Despite Godwin's protestations, however, the two—she a month less than seventeen, he a week less than twenty-two—accompanied by Claire Clairmont, eloped to the Continent on 28 July 1814; Godwin noted in his journal, "Five in the morning." Apparently Mary Shelley's "excessive" childhood affection for her father had been displaced by her love for P. B. Shelley and autonomy. But the significance of her parents' influence on both her and P. B. Shelley add unusual complexity to this elopement. Although she rebelled against the Godwin of 1814, she enacted a number of the ideals of Godwin—and Wollstonecraft—of the 1790s. Mary Shelley's letters following their return to England in September 1814 suggest genuine surprise that Godwin refused to accept their actions. Obviously pained by Godwin's refusal to see her, which lasted until the Shelleys were married in 1816, she blamed his rejection on her stepmother rather than on her beloved father and mentor. The love, adventure, and intellectual

idealism she shared with P. B. Shelley, however, overshad-
owed the loss of her father's approbation, making her all
the more independent.

In addition to Godwin, the three elopers left behind
many other distressed relatives: P. B. Shelley's wife, Harriet Shelley, caring for their child Ianthe Shelley (1813–76)
and expecting their second child, Charles Shelley (1814–
26); her father and sister; P. B. Shelley's father, Sir Timothy Shelley (1753–1844), and his family; and Mary Jane
Godwin, who rushed to Calais in an unsuccessful attempt
to convince her daughter to return home.[58]

But if the young people did not have Godwin's approval,
they had a kind of simulated parental approval in the works
of Mary Wollstonecraft that they took with them, *Letters from
Norway* and *Mary, A Fiction.*[59] In addition, they followed Godwin's practice of keeping a daily journal, quite likely finding in both books and journal-keeping tacit justification
for their actions. The journals, the first of the Shelleys'
many collaborations, eventually became Mary Shelley's responsibility.[60] In them she briefly noted their major daily
activities, including reading and writing. Mary Shelley also
brought with her "a box of her own writings—and letters,"[61]
and as they traveled the couple continued with their own
writing. There was yet another link to her parents: by the
time they returned to England, the unwed couple were expecting their first child. The Shelleys, then, had the same
kind of dual relationship Godwin and Wollstonecraft had
shared, a passion for each other and a passion for writing.

Their six weeks' tour took them through war-torn France, Switzerland, and Germany between Napoleon's first and second defeats. On their return to London in September 1814, they anticipated Sir Timothy's rejection, but they were surprised that their friends also shunned them.[62] And most unforeseen was Godwin's refusal to see his daughter. This was her first, and perhaps her most painful, introduction to the role "polite" society thereafter assigned her, as one who was "so entirely exiled from the good society of my own country on account of the outset of my life" and for whom life in England was a "prison house where humiliation, scorn & exile are my portion."[63]

The Shelleys' eight years together were dramatic and extraordinary. Their first child, a girl, born on 22 February 1815, died on 6 March. As a result of the death of P. B. Shelley's grandfather, Sir Bysshe Shelley, on 5 January 1815, they were rescued from poverty.[64] In accordance with a legal agreement with Sir Timothy Shelley, P. B. Shelley would receive an annual income of £1,000 plus additional sums to settle old debts. Free from financial restrictions, they were now able to establish a household in Bishopsgate (1815–16), where their second child, William Shelley, was born on 24 January 1816. In the summer of 1816 they traveled to Lake Geneva. This allowed Claire Clairmont to be near Lord Byron, the lover by whom she was already pregnant. After Byron rejected an ongoing liaison with Claire Clairmont, the Shelley entourage left Switzerland and returned to England. They lived first at Bath, where Allegra

Byron was born on 12 January 1817 (d. 1822), and then, from March 1817, at Albion House, Marlow, where the Shelleys' third child, Clara Everina, was born on 2 September. In February 1818 the Shelleys, Claire Clairmont, and the children moved to London, leaving England on 11 March for Italy, where their pattern of relocation would be frequently repeated. Mary Shelley integrated the same pattern in the plots of each of her six novels and one novella, representing physical transition as a key to her characters' struggles to relocate themselves psychologically and spiritually.

While they were in England, two other deaths altered the Shelleys' lives. In October 1816 the despondent Fanny Godwin committed suicide. This shock was followed by another in December 1816, when they learned that Harriet Shelley had drowned herself in the Thames.[65] The advice that legalizing their relationship would provide a better chance of gaining custody of Ianthe and Charles prompted Mary and P. B. Shelley to marry on 30 December 1816. Other reasons prompted it as well, including Godwin's strong wishes.[66] But P. B. Shelley, despite his own disparagement of marriage, also accepted the need for legal protection: he and Harriet Shelley had married a second time because false allegations of their ages on the first certificate had opened it to question.[67] Mary and P. B. Shelley's marriage brought reconciliation between Mary Shelley and Godwin but not guardianship of P. B. Shelley's first children. In March 1817 the Chancery Court denied P. B.

Shelley sole custody "upon the fact that in his case immoral opinions had led to conduct that the court was bound to consider immoral" and he would "inculcate similar opinions and conduct in his children,"[68] again reminding the Shelleys of their existence on the margins of society.

The Shelleys had, however, formed a circle of their own, which included Lord Byron, Thomas Love Peacock, Thomas Jefferson Hogg, Leigh and Marianne Hunt, and Claire Clairmont, who, to Mary Shelley's chagrin, often lived with them. And with the Shelleys' marriage, Mary Shelley could again have the company and counsel of her beloved father. What she could not have, however, was the friendship of her dear childhood friend Isabella Baxter Booth. Separated by Booth's family's disapproval of Mary Shelley's liaison with P. B. Shelley, they would not be reunited until after P. B. Shelley's death.[69]

During the Shelleys' time in England, Mary Shelley described their home as "very political as well as poetical."[70] In an atmosphere of mutual support and inspiration the two spent much of their time reading. The extensive book lists in Mary Shelley's journals illustrate the scope and depth of that reading, indicating which books both read, which one or the other read, and which P. B. Shelley read aloud to Mary Shelley and whomever else was present. P. B. Shelley, five years older than Mary Shelley and the beneficiary of private and Eton educations, introduced his own remarkable breadth of learning to his young partner, just as Godwin had extended P. B. Shelley's learning.[71]

Mary Shelley, an avid student, readily welcomed the opportunity for expanded learning. Continuing her Latin, she began to learn Greek, both languages serving in that era as the barrier between women and the era's definition of serious study: reading the classics in the original. To these and French she added Italian and some Spanish.

The Shelleys' journals and letters also indicate the collaborative nature of their intellectual relationship, which eventually included editing each other's works, translations, reacting and encouraging each other's writing, and contributing to the same projects.[72] Perhaps most important, their collaboration brought each a political, intellectual, and enthusiastic ally during years when Mary Shelley was developing her adult literary voice and P. B. Shelley's ideals, articulated in his works, were drawing critical scorn.

From the beginning, as Mary Shelley acknowledged, P. B. Shelley encouraged her to "obtain literary reputation, which even on my own part I cared for then, though since I have become infinitely indifferent to it."[73] His encouragement of her ambition was certainly one of the attractions that drew the pair together. While he wrote *Alastor* (1816) and *Laon and Cythna (The Revolt of Islam)* (1817), Mary Shelley wrote two anonymously published prose works, *History of a Six Weeks' Tour* and her masterpiece, *Frankenstein; or, the Modern Prometheus*. Both of these works subverted current genres, using accepted forms for other than their presumed purpose, in the interest of her reformist agenda.

History of a Six Weeks' Tour, published in November 1817,[74] is a reworking of the Shelleys' journal of their elopement tour through France, Switzerland, Germany, and Holland. Like the journal, *History of a Six Weeks' Tour* begins on 28 July 1814 and ends on 13 September, when, lacking money, they return to Gravesend. To this 1814 memoir are added four 1816 letters from Switzerland, two from each of the Shelleys, and P. B. Shelley's poem *Mont Blanc.* Their objective was "to journey towards the lake of Uri, and seek in that romantic and interesting country some cottage where we might dwell in peace and solitude" (*N&SW,* 8:29). But *History* and the letters are not merely a compilation of selections from the journal and their correspondence. Nor are they simple biographical narrative. Rather, although both offer some of the trappings of conventional travel diaries and correspondence, they shift the expected emphasis on observation and advice about travel to observation and advice about humanistic values. To an important degree, *History* establishes a philosophic perspective and a technique that would resonate in Mary Shelley's novels, in her last book *(Rambles),* and in many of her essays, as well as in the prefaces and notes to P. B. Shelley's works. The six most important aspects of that perspective and technique are:

1. consistent reformist belief in a social and personal code based not on power but on love and individual dignity;

2. purposive transformation, that is, she drew on accepted genres and beliefs, whether historical, scientific, social, political, literary, or gender-oriented, to draw in readers by

the familiar and then altered those stories to open the imagination, offering a metaphoric reworking that would lead readers to transform their own perspectives in support of (1) above;

3. actual biographical experience altered for purposes of metaphoric support of the work's philosophy;[75]

4. travel, as a means of enlarging perspectives and itself an apt metaphor for an agenda that calls for change;

5. a narrative told through the psychology of the individual, whose feelings and inner reflections interact with the external world;

6. education, as the means to achieve her reformist sociopolitical ends.

The preface to *History of a Six Weeks' Tour,* written by P. B. Shelley, introduces all six characteristics and subtly instructs the reader on how to approach and value the book. Based on an "imperfect journal and two or three letters," the story tells of a "desultory visit by a party of young people"—the author, her husband, and her sister—who travel on foot, pursuing "like the swallow, the inconstant summer of delight and beauty which invests this visible world." The travelers are unconventional from the start: women who travel on foot, looking for "delight and beauty" rather than the customary tourist quest for art and culture found in major cities. Adding to the unconventionality, their journey through war-torn Europe allows for reformist commentary on the politics and devastation of war. Beyond seeing other parts of the world, they follow and imitate the unconstrained, natural movements of the swallow, thereby freeing themselves from the restrictions, personal and societal, of prevailing mores and laws.

In the same spirit, the narrative expresses the personal feelings of the travelers about people and circumstances, suggesting to the reader how he or she too should respond. Furthermore, despite the anonymity of the author, the book's references to "S***" and "C***" certainly informed the small circle of literate London whom the book was by and about, for the story of the Shelleys'—and Claire Clairmont's—elopement was a favorite of gossips, and remained so for the rest of Mary Shelley's life.[76] *History of a Six Weeks' Tour,* pre-announced as a travel journal, actually offers the reader a model of how to approach travel—and life—from the Shelleyan Romantic perspective.

Travel journals in epistolary format, published and private, were a popular genre of the time. Beyond Godwin's own daily journal, *History of a Six Weeks' Tour* and "Letters of . . . Geneva" had a closer, more compelling influence: Mary Wollstonecraft's epistolary travelogue, *Letters from Norway,* which the party read en route.[77] Wollstonecraft's work is a singular blend of sociopolitical reformist perspectives and personal melancholia, though the reason for that melancholia is unspoken. Typical of travel literature, *Letters from Norway* includes practical commentary about inhabitants, transportation, lodgings, and food. These details would particularly interest Wollstonecraft's readers because the book surveys a part of the world then relatively unknown to the British. Wollstonecraft's travelogue is compelling, however, as a result of her remarkable topographical musings, which reflect on politics, society, aesthetics, and her own feelings. The work provided Mary Shelley with a perfect model, by an idealized mentor, of disguised early Romantic commentary as well as genre subversion.

Not that Mary Shelley required a secondhand appreciation of travel and its inherent capacity to expand the imagination. Her eight-month sojourn in 1811 at Ramsgate and her year and a half between 1812 and 1814 in Scotland, where she had an "eyry of freedom" in which she could commune with "the creatures of my fancy" (*N&SW*, 1:176), had already awakened her to the advantages of separation from commonplace restraints, both familial and societal, as well as a love for travel. Travel would provide her, as it did P. B. Shelley and Byron, with excitement, inspiration, separation from an inhospitable London, and relative freedom from social constraint. The latter, for a woman, was particularly welcome given England's postwar conservative disposition.

The journal contains comments about "unamiable" French, filthy inns, inedible food, typical of nineteenth-century tourist diaries.[78] But *History of a Six Weeks' Tour* instead emphasizes descriptions favorable to the French, and often unfavorable to the English: "the manners and appearance of the people of Calais, that prepossesses you in their favour" (*N&SW*, 8:16); "The lower orders in France have the easiness and politeness of the most well-bred English; they treat you unaffectedly as their equal, and consequently there is no scope for insolence" (8:17); "The first appearance that struck our English eyes was the want of enclosures; but the fields were flourishing with a plentiful harvest" (8:17). Politically pointed, these accolades underscore the link between the 1814 defeated enemy of Britain and the pre-Napoleon democratic spirit of the 1789 Revolution, a spirit the Shelleys wished to reactivate.

The detestation of war and the concern for the abuse of power that one sees in her novels may well have been first inspired by their visit to Nogent,

> entirely desolated by the Cossacs. Nothing could be more entire than the ruin which these barbarians had spread as they advanced; perhaps they remembered Moscow and the destruction of the Russian villages; but we were now in France, and the distress of the inhabitants . . . has given a sting to my detestation of war, which none can feel who have not travelled through a country pillaged and wasted by this plague, which, in his pride, man inflicts upon his fellow. (8:21)

In the transformation of the private journal into the public work her observation no longer pertains that at Echemines the people were so unamiable that they "could hardly pity" their ruin at the hands of the Cossacks.[79]

History of a Six Weeks' Tour celebrates nature in its variegated shades and proportions. Unenclosed and unexpected, its visible manifestations are at times associated with the metaphysical, as when the immensity of the Alps "staggers the imagination, and so far surpasses all conception, that it requires an effort of the understanding to believe that they indeed form a part of the earth" (*N&SW*, 8:28), a description she selected from P. B. Shelley's journal entries.

Mary Shelley's narrative, like Wollstonecraft's, is skillfully defiant. In contrast to the prevalent genre approach, she includes references to the travelers' readings, which reflect erudition as well as a liberal political bias unexpected for a woman at the time. In addition to Wollstonecraft's *Letters from Norway,* they read the *Siege of Jerusalem* from Tacitus; the third canto of Byron's *Childe Harold;* and Latin and Italian. One might expect to find opinions about locals and their customs, manners, lodgings, and scenery in a travelogue, but not the assessment of politics and war, subjects considered inappropriate for women. Their perspectives brought both Wollstonecraft and Mary Shelley the equivocal compliment that they possessed "masculine" understanding.[80] In publishing her own travel narrative, Mary Shelley continued her mother's vocation as reformist educator, itself a rebellious stance for women.

If the travelers denigrate members of the lower classes in *History of a Six Weeks' Tour,* the blame lies not with the inherent characters of the latter but with their conditions, reflecting the Shelleys' belief that the sociopolitical system coarsened the poor just as it corrupted the rich. Such concepts, together with the book's sympathetic delineation of the French, made the publication of *History of a Six Weeks' Tour* in

1817 a bold reminder of the egalitarian ideals of the French Revolution in a Europe in which "the great conspiracy of kings" had re-established its control.[81]

Politicized themes of power and responsibility, enunciated in a *History of a Six Weeks' Tour,* are central to *Frankenstein,* written before the shorter work but published at the beginning of January 1818.[82] The complexities of *Frankenstein,* its own three authorial texts of 1818, 1823,[83] and 1831, plus the many translations, the early and late prefaces, and its blend of the Gothic and the Godwinian psychological, sociopolitical novel with Mary Shelley's own particular Romanticist sensibility, open it to many possible readings, among them Gothic, political, biographical, religious, psychological, anti-male feminist, anti-Godwin and anti-Shelley. From its initial publication, and increasingly in the last two decades, these multiple interpretations have often contradicted one another, dealt only with certain facets of the book, or attributed to Mary Shelley concepts that have more to do with the bias of the particular critic than with the author herself. Despite the variations, however, there is a thread that ties them together: to differing degrees, they reflect Mary Shelley's consistent, larger metaphoric question of the exercise of power and responsibility, personal and societal.

In her 1831 introduction Mary Shelley described the genesis of the novel (*N&SW,* 1:175). The Shelleys, Lord Byron, and John Polidori, Byron's physician, after an evening of reading ghost stories,[84] agreed that each would

write a terrifying tale. But if the immediate impetus was literary, Mary Shelley, influenced by Godwin and Wollstonecraft's Enlightenment agenda,[85] reinforced by her life with
P. B. Shelley, extended the literary into political questions
of power and justice. The conversations of P. B. Shelley
and Byron that summer, to which Mary Shelley, according
to her description, was mostly a listener, were clearly as
much about politics as about literature. In a sense, even the
story writing was a contest about power: recognized authors
Byron and P. B. Shelley vying with the untried Mary Shelley and Polidori. That Mary Shelley agreed to participate
and then day after day felt frustrated at not coming up with
a topic reflected her own self-expectations, as did her apparent satisfaction when she announced to P. B. Shelley
the morning after her famous nightmare that "I had *thought
of a story*" and "began that day with the words, *It was on a dreary
night of November.*" In the course of the writing, at P. B. Shelley's encouragement, the story became a full-length novel
in which traditional Gothic characteristics that blended
mystery and horror within an emphasis on setting and plot
were subsumed within a politicized emphasis on character
and psychological struggle.

Frankenstein plays out the exploration of power on four
different narrative levels, in form, story within story within
story, iterating human interdependency however accidental
or unrecognized: first, the letters from the seafarer Robert
Walton to his sister Margaret Walton Saville, which form
the outer frame for his particular story as well as for the

other narratives; second, the scientist Victor Frankenstein's telling of his version of the history of his creation and abandonment of, and death struggle with, the Creature; third, the incorporation of the Creature's version of his abandonment, his desperate loneliness, and his transformation from good to evil as he mirrors his creator's values; and fourth, the Felix-and-Safie tale of heroism, injustice, and love told within the Creature's story. To these one might add a larger outer frame: the unknown reader, escorted through Dantean circles of terror and pity, led on by the seductive attraction of reading letters addressed to someone else.

The interconnection of the levels by the delivery of the stories mirrors the likeness of the stories themselves: Walton, in his ambition to discover a new polar route, fantasizes about "the inestimable benefit which I shall confer on all mankind to the last generation" (*N&SW*, 1:10), acting out an applied, secular exploration, whereas Frankenstein's quest for the secret of life is on a metaphysical and theoretical scale. In the end it is Walton who changes, forced "in justice" to place the wishes of the community (the sailors on his ship) above his own ambitions. Felix's story initially demonstrates the injustice of the established system of government. When a Turkish merchant long resident in Paris is unjustly jailed and sentenced to death, Felix heroically rescues him. Caught, Felix's punishment, extended to his family as well, is loss of all possessions and exile. The foreigner adds to his suffering by breaking his promise that his daughter Safie and Felix would marry. But this tale ends in Felix's own act of injustice. When he sees the Creature, who has been secretly bringing food and firewood to the cottagers, rather than asking his story, as Felix's blind father does, he violently attacks him. Through this act, Felix is no longer simply a victim of the sociopolitical power structure; he is also its agent.

Safie's story, like Felix's, at first also suggests humanitarian values not in keeping with the contemporary European systems of government. Her deceased mother, a "Christian Arab" rescued from slavery through marriage to Safie's father, "instructed her daughter in the tenets of her religion, and taught her to aspire to higher powers of intellect, and an independence of spirit, forbidden to the female followers of Mahomet." Safie, "now accustomed to grand ideas and a noble emulation for virtue," defies her father. Taking her jewels, she joins Felix and his family, repulsed by the thought of living mindlessly in a harem compared with the enchanting "prospect of marrying a Christian, and remaining in a country where women were allowed to take a rank in society" (*N&SW*, 1:92). But her escape from one kind of injustice fails to teach her not to perpetrate another. Safie reacts to the Creature by running from the cottage, not even stopping to assist Felix's sister Agatha, who has fainted. Her self-centered reaction is a far cry from her abstract notion of the "higher powers of intellect, and an independence of spirit" that a woman could pursue in Christian Europe; rather, she becomes a parody of her potential idealism, failing just as Frankenstein, Felix, and, inevitably, the Creature fail.

As in Dante's and Milton's epics, on which Mary Shelley drew, the multiple layers of *Frankenstein* present a variety of visions, but in contrast to epic narrative, Mary Shelley presents no stable, reliable narrator. Instead, the reader alone must evaluate the validity of a character's words and actions. In sum, we are given Frankenstein's loving father, who nevertheless fails to educate his son properly; his mother, who, in accordance with the social norms, abdicates all responsibility for the education of her son; Elizabeth, Frankenstein's fiancee, who also adheres to the social norms, though she does undergo a change in which she loses first her faith in the justice system and then her life, victimized directly and indirectly by Frankenstein's code; Clerval, a poet, murdered because of his best friend; Justine, a servant, forced to confess to a murder she did not commit and then hanged for it; Frankenstein himself, a wealthy, indulged young man whose acceptance of his society's norms leads him to want, like a monarch or a god, absolute power and, whatever his disastrous experience, makes him incapable of understanding his inherent error and accountability; and a very unheroic-appearing Creature, who goes from a state of natural goodness to one of crime and transgression but fully understands and assumes responsibility for the horrors of his deeds, though he is incapable of restraining himself.

By subtitling her novel "The Modern Prometheus" Mary Shelley configures her story in the shadow of Prometheus's act of bringing knowledge to humankind, concretizing the issue through examples of educational practices and their failure throughout the novel. But in her purposive transformation of the older myth of enlightenment, with its expected benefit to humanity, she has created a new and dangerous story that challenges the rationale behind Victor Frankenstein's quest and his intended "gift." In the Greek myth, the result of Prometheus's actions, like Christ's, is redemptive suffering for humanity. Frankenstein's quest, conversely, reveals itself to be more for the attainment of personal, godlike power than for societal advancement. In this reversal of expectation Frankenstein becomes the first of a number of unheroic male central figures in Mary Shelley's fiction. A failed Prometheus, he suffers not for humankind but for his own unprincipled judgment, and not willingly. This modern Prometheus, then, reduces the "heroic" act to a mocking parody of enlightenment intention and execution.

The personification of that parody is the Creature, a Rousseauian natural savage who evolves from a condition of instinctual goodness to learned evil, mirroring a society based on fear and more a bona fide member of that society than he ever realizes. A fundamental expectation of danger and attack inherent in systems based on power leads to a prevalent fear of the other. The Creature, as constructed by Mary Shelley, is the living metaphor of that other and as such expresses the position of anyone viewed as an outsider. As the Creature educates himself first through contact with nature, then through the works of Milton, Plutarch, Volney, and Goethe, and language itself, his thoughts and actions argue for the value of the Shelleys' amalgam of reason and love. When he breaks from this model and emulates the power system prevalent in the nineteenth century, he, like his creator, becomes both victim and perpetuator of that system.

Frankenstein, then, may be seen as a republican form of the Prometheus myth. Power, in this telling, is in the hands of mortals, who also have the capability to bring light to their own civilization. The issue in *Frankenstein* is not, as is so often repeated in traditional religious arguments, a lesson in the dangers of the usurpation of God's domain. Rather, consistent with Mary Shelley's reformist ideology, the novel proposes that whether a Prometheus or a Frankenstein usurps power, the result may be good or evil. In questioning the very idea of power as an instrument of God, Mary Shelley suggests that unjust social conditions can be interpreted as the work not of God but rather of humanity itself and therefore are subject to change.

Contemporary religious traditionalists were certainly aware of this implication, and a number of the reviews expressly addressed the issue. Suspicious of this Godwinian novel, they asserted that *Frankenstein* was a lesson in the dangers of attempting to usurp God's power or noted, within the same context, that it bordered on blasphemy (see *N&SW*, vol. I, introductory note). In translating the novel on its surface level, the establishment inflected it to serve their conservative ideology. This misreading of the novel's reformist idealism, subtly supported in the negative scenario of *Frankenstein* as it was in Godwin's *Caleb Williams* and Wollstonecraft's *Maria,* nullifies the objectives of the novel and its author.

Traditionalists have applied the same conservative reading to the instruments of that implied usurpation: science and technology. But this facile conclusion is inconsistent with the overall philosophy that informs *Frankenstein,* Mary Shelley's other works, as well as her letters. Science from Copernicus and Galileo, incorporated into the theories of Newton, shifted the understanding of the universe from a blend of the natural and supernatural to the mechanistic vision at the very center of the Enlightenment philosophy. If objects no longer have the essence of God in them, then any shape or essence is possible and the search for that essence becomes a means towards communal and individual self-definition. Just as one branch of knowledge sought to define the laws of scientific nature, another might lead to uncovering the laws of social nature, a theory that strongly influenced reformers of the period, including the Godwin-Shelley circle.[86]

For the Shelleys, therefore, scientific experimentation served as a paradigm for political experimentation: both offered the means to create a better world. P. B. Shelley's

own strong interest in science[87] may have motivated Mary
Shelley, during the writing of *Frankenstein,* to read the works
of Sir Humphry Davy, a pioneer of galvanic electricity.[88] As
the 1818 and 1831 introductions attest, P. B. Shelley's conversations with Lord Byron brought the evolutionary theories of Erasmus Darwin to Mary Shelley's attention in the
early phase of writing the novel.[89] But the theories of Darwin and Davy may have been familiar to her much earlier
since both men were friends of Godwin's.[90] Furthermore,
it is possible that Mary Shelley may have had some tutelage
in science generally through some of Godwin's close association with his admired friend William Nicholson, whom
Godwin "turned to for information on the latest theories
in chemistry, physics, optics, biology, and other natural
sciences."[91]

Far from condemning scientific exploration, Mary Shelley adopted this major enthusiasm in England at the time
as a germane metaphor through which to examine age-old
political inequities.[92] For example, the idea of discovering
"the secret of the magnet" through polar exploration was
an important scientific quest in this period. In 1600 William Gilbert had discovered that the earth itself is a great
magnet, with a north and a south magnetic pole, and the-
orized on the principles of "electrical attraction."[93] Gilbert
also tied magnetism to the life force itself: "Magnetick
force is animate, or imitates life; and in many things surpasses human life, while this is bound up in the organick
body."[94] Thus, the scientific basis of Walton's goal to reach

the North Pole is directly associated with Frankenstein's goal of formulating human life, which in turn derives from the experiments in electricity and reanimation of Luigi Galvani (1737–98) and Alessandro Volta (1745–1827).

The conservative appropriation of the novel as a warning against scientific research, like the conservative religious reading of *Frankenstein,* continues to this day to deflect the novel's reformist intentions. Within the terms of the novel, Frankenstein's limitation is not that he enters sacred realms but that he fails to take responsibility for his own actions. Akin to P. B. Shelley's Alastor, who also delves in "charnels and coffins" (line 24)[95] and perishes a victim of self-centeredness, Frankenstein fails to reach beyond himself. The Creature recognizes this defect when he draws on his reading of *Paradise Lost* to compare how he is different from Satan, whose goal was power. The Creature's plea is one of many calls to awaken Frankenstein that go unheard: "I ought to be thy Adam; but I am rather the fallen angel, whom thou drivest from joy for no misdeed . . . . I was benevolent and good; misery made me a fiend. Make me happy, and I shall again be virtuous" (*N&SW,* 1:74).

But Frankenstein remains locked in his insular world. He is not alone, however, in suffering the furies that beset his failed Promethean quest. His actions destroy the larger community, including his young brother William, Justine, Elizabeth, and Clerval. Frankenstein's failure, then, is a parable for the failure of the nineteenth-century sociopolitical structure to take responsibility—material and spir-

itual—for the greater populace. The novel iterates the
Godwinian-Wollstonecraft concept that a corrupt system
will taint or destroy all its inhabitants, expressed in their
philosophic tracts *Political Justice* and *Vindication* and then fic-
tionalized in the novels *Caleb Williams* and *Maria. Frankenstein*
resurrects these eighteenth-century theories in a model
that offers its nineteenth-century audience, now shifted
from revolutionary war to revolutionary commerce and industry, the possibility of making responsible choices.

Frankenstein's choice in assembling and then responding to the Creature serves as a paradigm for individuals and
societies as they newly assemble their society of their own
"component parts." This is the connotation of the novel's
epigraph, which raises the question of responsibility of
both creator and created:

> Did I request thee, Maker, from my clay
> To mold me man? Did I solicit thee
> From darkness to promote me?—
>
>   *(Paradise Lost* 10.743–45)

The characters of Frankenstein and the Creature, as well as
their relationship, bring into question what and how we
see; how we are conditioned to see; and, not least of all,
how we create.

The novel shifts the role of the artist-creator, Frankenstein as well as Mary Shelley, from observer and commen-
tator to shaper. *Frankenstein,* through its author, interpolates
the woman as the creator, who comments on a failed socio-

political system engineered and controlled by men. It also aligns her with visionary political reformers—among them her parents and P. B. Shelley—who embraced the Enlightenment belief in the potential improvement of humanity.

In representing a world in chaos Mary Shelley reflects the world around her. The Creature's desire for connection also reflects that world as it experiences, however willingly, increasing disassociation with past traditions and structures. The Creature's desire for friendship and education also reflect Mary Shelley's personal values, which oppose Frankenstein's, for whom human relationships are a matter of convenience, to be set aside in his quest for power. Chaos becomes both systemic and personal in the novel. In her metaphoric exploration of the bleak realities of society Mary Shelley poses the possibility of wresting order from chaos. But it is not a simple, utopian or romance-novel resolution. Byron's Don Juan exclaims, "I want a Hero!" In fact, the absence of a hero is integral to *Frankenstein* in its model of power without responsibility. Rather than offering an easy moral, the novel offers complex choices, epitomized by its conclusion. The tormented Creature, agonizing at Frankenstein's deathbed about responsibility, love, and guilt, vows to "collect my funeral pile, and consume to ashes this miserable frame" (*N&SW*, 1:169). But *Frankenstein* offers no confirmation that this pledge is enacted.

For Mary Shelley, the remedy to the destructive values presented in *Frankenstein* was to be found in Enlightenment theory, which argued for universal education, united with Shelleyan love, as the evolutionary means to benevolent social structures for the common good. In an 1823 letter she made clear her own educational intentions for that novel: "I own I have great respect for that faculty we carry about us called Mind—and I fear that no Frankenstein can so arrange the gases as to be able to make any combination of them produce thought or even life—However happy conjectures must always instruct even if they fail from entirely attaining their object."[96] Perhaps this is the reason *Frankenstein,* in its metaphoric interrogation of transition and values, intrigued so many readers in its own day and continues to in our own time.

CHAPTER TWO

Italy, 1818–1823

EVEN as the reviews of *Frankenstein* appeared in the press, the Shelleys left England (on 11 March 1818) to begin their peripatetic life in Italy. From April 1818, when they arrived at Milan, to July 1822 they lived in Leghorn, Bagni di Lucca, Venice, Este, Naples, Rome, Florence, Pisa, Bagni di Pisa, and finally San Terenzo, their last home together. As they traveled, their friendships expanded: Jane and Edward Williams, Edward John Trelawny, Emilia Viviani, Thomas Medwin, Maria and John Gisborne, Mr. and Mrs. Mason (Mr. George Tighe and the former Lady Mount Cashell), were all present at different times and played a variety of roles, sometimes closer to one or the other Shelley, sometimes distant from both.

At the same time, the complexity of their own relationship increased. P. B. Shelley's philosophy of expansive rather than exclusive love periodically led him to auxiliary objects of love and inspiration. Although tensions about other women may have caused jealousy in the marriage, Mary Shelley's own belief in expansive love led her to recognize those women on their own terms, and her judgments about them should be evaluated accordingly. These women include Claire Clairmont; the unidentified mother of "the Neapolitan child," Elena Adelaide Shelley, the baby at first secretly registered by P. B. Shelley as his and Mary Shelley's;[1] as well as Sophia Stacey, Emilia Viviani, and Jane Williams. P. B. Shelley's "best Mary" was aware of his feelings and reacted to what appeared to be temporary interests in different ways. Just as Mary Shelley had been encouraged by P. B. Shelley in 1814 to attempt an "expansive" love relationship, with Hogg,[2] she had her own unconventional response to P. B. Shelley's attentions to these women as she herself formed special friendships with several of the Shelleys' male friends, including Prince Alexander Mavrocordato and Edward Williams.

Mary Shelley's letters and journals provide evidence that Mary Shelley also befriended Stacey, Viviani, and Jane Williams and exhibit how her feelings at times diverged from P. B. Shelley's. For example, her letters make clear that initially she was as intrigued as P. B. Shelley with Viviani. Her disenchantment with Viviani appears to have arisen not from jealousy but from a far earlier perception than P. B. Shelley's of the triviality of Viviani's character.[3] Years later Mary Shelley captured that character in her short story "The Bride of Modern Italy," even repeating Viviani's own statement about herself that she "changed saints every time she changed lovers."[4]

Her initial attitude towards Jane Williams was much like P. B. Shelley's. She described Jane Williams as "very pretty" but wanting in "animation and sense; her conversation is *nothing particular,* and she speaks in a slow monotonous voice: but she appears good tempered and tolerant."[5] P. B. Shelley initially described her as "an extremely pretty & gentle woman—apparently not *very* clever. I like her very much"; a half-year later he wrote, "I have got reconciled to Jane." Another half-year would pass before he described her as "more amiable and beautiful than ever, and a sort of spirit of embodied peace in our circle of tempests. So much for first impressions!"[6]

The one woman against whom Mary Shelley reacted most strongly and complexly in her life with P. B. Shelley, and afterwards, was her stepsister. From the time of the elopement Claire Clairmont had been an almost permanent member of the household. Increasingly, Clairmont's friendship with P. B. Shelley and her general demands on their time and energy irritated Mary Shelley to the point that she told P. B. Shelley, "give me a garden & *absentia Clariæ* and I will thank my love for many favours."[7] A number of critics believe that P. B. Shelley and Clairmont's relationship was sexual in nature and have promoted the unsubstantiated rumor that they were the parents of the "Neapolitan child," which both Shelleys strongly denied.[8] Rumors and Mary Shelley's antipathy notwithstanding, she accepted Claire Clairmont as family and the two women remained friends and sparring partners until almost the end of Mary Shelley's life.[9]

It is always difficult to understand the tides of relationships from an observer's perspective—and even from a participant's. But certainly two closely linked tragedies threatened the Shelleys' union. On 24 September 1818 one-year-old Clara Everina Shelley died of dysentery at Venice.[10] The Shelleys were bereft. Then, on 7 June 1819 William Shelley, almost three and a half, succumbed to malaria. The devastated Mary Shelley wrote, "I never know one moments ease from the wretchedness & despair that possesses me—May you my dear Marianne never know what it is to lose two only & lovely children in one year—to watch their dying moments—& then at last to be left childless & for ever miserable."[11]

Both Shelleys deeply mourned their loss, but for Mary Shelley the deaths of their children seemed an insurmountable grief. Just as in 1816, when she half-apologetically teased P. B. Shelley about wanting another baby,[12] she makes clear over and again in her letters and journals that she was not the unwilling sexual and maternal partner she has sometimes been made out to be, that her children were crucial to her life. She writes that she "ought to have died on the 7th of June last" (William's death) and goes so far as to say she would rather have forgone her years with P. B. Shelley than "cruelly have lost the associations of four years."[13]

One may speculate that the two children for her represented more than her union with P. B. Shelley, and more than renewal after her first lost child. Quite possibly a primary motivation, conscious or not, in Mary Shelley's strong desire to have children related to her own mother's life and death. Perhaps through the deliberate acts of bearing and rearing children she celebrated and forgave both her mother and herself for her own birth at the same time that she forgave Wollstonecraft's death, which had left her motherless. With her own children she secured mother-child affection that she may have imagined would have been hers had Mary Wollstonecraft lived and in this idolization further cleared her mother's name of the slurs that adhered to it.

The intensity of her losses caused Mary Shelley to distance P. B. Shelley from her. During this period of estrangement the Shelleys' most harmonious communication appears to have been through their writing. After Clara's death, P. B. Shelley began to dramatize *The Cenci*. This widely known, underground story of the sixteenth-century Cenci family depicts the vicious cruelty of Count Francesco Cenci, whose wealth protected him from punishment for murdering his own sons and raping Beatrice, his daughter. After the rape, Beatrice conspired with other family members to murder him. Victims first of Cenci's unlimited power, then of the Church's, Beatrice and her co-conspirators were caught and executed. The Shelleys col-

laborated on this project in several ways. Mary Shelley
translated into English "Relazione della morte della fami-
glia Cenci sequita in Roma il di II Maggio 1599," the original Italian manuscript from which P. B. Shelley worked,
for intended publication with P. B. Shelley's tragedy.[14] She
also indicated that this was the only work of P. B. Shelley's
that he discussed with her part by part as he wrote it.

Following William's death, as P. B. Shelley continued
working on *The Cenci*, Mary Shelley began her own story of
incest: *Matilda*, the story of a father's annihilating incestuous love for his daughter.[15] In its subject of incest and its
use of sexual metaphor to play out the theme of power and
failed responsibility, *Matilda* was a continuation of the Shelleys' *The Cenci* collaboration in the midst of their emotional
estrangement. As I have suggested elsewhere, these writings
may also have served as a gesture of personal reconciliation
between the couple[16] rather than, as some critics have suggested, a subjective expression of Mary Shelley's anger at
P. B. Shelley or at Godwin.

Matilda's story is less extreme than that of *The Cenci* or the
distancing supernatural plot of *Frankenstein*. The father is
neither rapist nor murderer but a wealthy scion whose indulged upbringing fails to develop values in him beyond
his own self-interest. De-villainized, his actions become
more plausible and therefore more realistic and dangerous. With no name in the story other than "father," he
symbolizes the generic idea of an authority figure, parent,
monarch, or god who fails in his responsibility towards his

dependents. The device of not naming in *Frankenstein* leads the reader from abhorrence to sympathy for the Creature, shifting the abhorrence to the scientist. In *Matilda,* readers are prompted to reject the "father," who in his socialization resembles Frankenstein. But as in the earlier work, neither of the two main figures in *Matilda* is heroic. Just as the basic theme of *Matilda* is consistent with the central theme of Mary Shelley's other longer works, so too is the character for whom it is titled. The only title character of one of Mary Shelley's longer works who is a female, Mathilda, like the Creature and, later, Perkin Warbeck, Lodore, and Falkner, is both victim of and accessory to a sociopolitical system premised on power and self-aggrandizement rather than on humanitarian values.

When Mathilda's mother dies in giving birth to her, her father leaves her to be raised by a cold and restrictive aunt while he, self-indulgently, wanders the world. Mathilda's education is intellectually and emotionally narrow, and in her loneliness she idolizes her absent father: "My favorite vision was that when I grew up I would leave my aunt, whose coldness lulled my conscience, and disguised like a boy I would seek my father through the world" (*N&SW,* 2:14). When he does return sixteen years later, he finds a lovely young woman, who he later confesses "appeared as the deity of a lovely region, the ministering Angel of a Paradise to which of all human kind you admitted only me" (2:33). After a brief idyll in which Mathilda and her father appear to achieve the parent-child relationship for which she always yearned, her father becomes depressed and distant as he recognizes his own "guilty love more unnatural than hate" (2:35). Deficient in character, he allows himself to be cajoled by Mathilda's naive importuning to reveal the cause of his anguish and admits his incestuous love to her. At her shock and rejection, he commits suicide.

Like the Creature, who argued that he should have been Frankenstein's Adam, Mathilda asserts that she was "ruthlessly driven" from "Paradisaical bliss," although "I disobeyed no command, I ate no apple. . . . Alas! my companion did, and I was precipitated in his fall" (2:17). Neither Mathilda's confined upbringing nor her conventional religion offers her the means to survive the tragedy or the guilt associated with her father's revelation and subsequent suicide. Despite her friend Woodville's valiant attempts to lead her to develop a more mature, independent relationship to herself and the world, she cannot free herself of her father's shattering control and fulfills her own death legacy.

Matilda represents Mary Shelley's alignment with other Romantics, as well as earlier illustrious authors including Sophocles, Euripides, and Dante, in treating the incest taboo.[17] Contemporary works about incest include P. B. Shelley's *Laon and Cythna*, Hunt's *Story of Rimini*, various works by Byron,[18] Godwin's *Mandeville*, and Mary Shelley's incomplete translation of Alfieri's *Myrra*.[19] When Hunt's *Rimini* was attacked in *Blackwood's Magazine*, it was for its sentimentalization of incest compared with prior treatments in which the consequence of incest was punishment. By this criterion, both *Cenci* and *Matilda* would have "passed" social standards. Years later, Mary Shelley's comments on Alfieri's *Myrra,* used as a pivotal point in *Matilda,* offer an insight into her view of incest as a literary subject. She writes of *Myrra,* "This is the fault of the subject; inequality of age adding to the unnatural incest. To shed any interest over such an attachment, the dramatist ought to adorn the father with such youthful attributes as would be by no means contrary to probability: but then a worse evil would ensue; and the more possible such criminal passion becomes, the more violently does the mind revolt from dwelling on it."[20]

Godwin's refusal to publish *Matilda* when Mary Shelley sent it to him from Italy has been interpreted to reflect Mary Shelley's actual feelings for her father, or his for her. Either case assumes that the novella was autobiographical or at the least that Godwin considered it as such. In contrast, neither P. B. Shelley nor Hunt has been the object of such narrow, biographical interpretation. The assumption that a female writer must personally experience a subject to write about it suggests that Mary Shelley was also a murderer or a warrior or lived in America or drowned at sea, as did the central characters in her other novels. There are two other far more probable reasons why neither Godwin nor Mary Shelley on her return to England published *Matilda.* First, Godwin feared that a work by Mary Shelley about incest might again stir rumors about the purportedly incestuous relationship between Mary Shelley, P. B. Shelley, and Claire Clairmont that arose when the three left England on their six weeks' tour, as suggested by one reviewer of an 1821 reprint of *Queen Mab*.[21] Second, Mary Shelley on her return to England had to contend with the social mores of the period, designed to restrict topics about which women could write in order to prevent a "wandering imagination which stepped out of all legitimate bounds."[22] Reviews of *Frankenstein* questioned the politics and religious implications of its subject but initially assumed, as did Walter Scott, that its author was a man.[23] In 1826, however, reviewers of *The Last Man* knew its author's identity and generally condemned the novel as beyond the pale for its effective depictions of death and disease (see *N&SW*, vol. 4, introductory note). Though incest was a "spiritual" rather than a legal crime in early-nineteenth-century England, occasionally grounds were found to prosecute.[24] A novella about incest by a woman, even if a publisher could be found, would be regarded as being "out of all legitimate bounds," bringing new scandal to the Shelley-Godwin circle. One almost certain result would be Mary Shelley's loss of Percy Florence Shelley to Sir Timothy Shelley, who from the outset had wanted total custody. Godwin's and Mary Shelley's own reason for not publishing *Matilda* was far less likely owing to fear of imputed incestuous feelings between them than to the recognition that for a woman, even one who had "masculine understanding," the subject of incest was simply not acceptable and would incur painful consequences.

In *Matilda,* Mary Shelley's purposive transformation
works on several levels to support her thesis of social responsibility: wealth and privilege, without appropriate education, are shown to breed narcissistic and destructive
behavior; the act of writing is offered as a dependable sub-
stitution for the act of prayer as a means of redemption;
and the work's reference to the Oedipus myth (*N&SW,* 2:5),
both in its incest theme and in its reflection of Oedipus's
determination to know the truth, rewrites the ancient
tragedy in contemporary terms.

In her journal Mary Shelley wrote: "When I wrote Matilda, miserable as I was, the inspiration was sufficient to
quell my wretchedness temporarily."[25] The writing of *Matilda* represented for its author a means of solace derived
from the empowering exercise of the imagination. In its
secularization of the religious loss-redemption model the
prayer ritual is replaced by that of writing. Throughout the
novella, Mathilda and Woodville reflexively refer to writing. Woodville's poetry transfigures him into the role of
self-minister. It enables him to reach beyond his own grief
to validate life itself: "when reason could no longer guide
him, his imagination as if inspired shed light on the ob-
scurity that veils the past and the future" (*N&SW,* 2:52).
Woodville epitomizes the Shelleyan Romantics' "power" of
mind to create "another world more lovely than the visible
frame of things, even all the world that we find in their
writings" (2:52). Thus, it is the writer who is the creator.
Mathilda, hardened by her responses to her father's trans-

gression and suicide, achieves a kind of redemption through her last act, the confessional writing of her story, in the end rejecting the "silence" in which she was schooled by her aunt and then, even more painfully, by her father.

Matilda, which is about death from beginning to end, reflects the loss of the Shelleys' children but argues that death, "instead of purifying the heart . . . is so intense a misery that it hardens & dulls the feelings" (2:66). In writing *Matilda,* Mary Shelley modeled how the imagination, which she always regarded as a special preserve, offered readers—and authors—objectivity and renewal. Through imagination one can re-see the world, a central philosophy in all of Mary Shelley's works, particularly in *The Last Man.*

Perhaps it was that renewal, and the birth of Percy Florence Shelley on 12 November 1819, that motivated her to move forward with a historical novel that she had thought about as early as 1817 and gave new shape to in early 1819 (see *N&SW,* vol. 3, introductory note). *Valperga; or, The Life and Adventures of Castruccio, Prince of Lucca* drew on her extensive research in Italian political history and literature, which she transposed to express her republican reformist philosophy.[26]

At the beginning of *Valperga,* civil war in 1301 between the Guelphs and the Ghibellines has nearly destroyed Lombardy and Tuscany. The Guelphs, in this cycle ascendant, force the Ghibellines into exile from Lucca. The eleven-year-old Castruccio and his family, who are Ghibellines, fear for their possessions and their lives. They are offered rescue by Antonio dei Adimari, a Guelph Florentine but a friend of Castruccio's father. Adimari sends his servant to conduct them to Valperga, his castle symbolically situated in the Apennines partway between Lucca, the Ghibelline stronghold, and Florence, the Guelph republic. There, Castruccio would have been reunited with Adimari's daughter Euthanasia, the future countess of Valperga and his beloved childhood friend. The relationship between Euthanasia and Castruccio, which with maturity grows into deep love, connotes, as does Valperga itself, the possibility of mediating the decades-long enmity between the warring parties. But in reality that promise never existed; nor did Euthanasia. In introducing a fictional heroic figure, Mary Shelley rewrote history to construct a paradigm for the resolution of factionalism, Italian or British, in the interest of the common good.

Castruccio, who like the Creature in *Frankenstein* begins as a sensitive, caring being, is consumed by hatred because of his family's exile. Schooled as a soldier in intrigue and machination, he becomes a fierce and powerful partisan of Ghibelline conquest. His brutality inevitably puts him in conflict with Euthanasia, a student of Latin history and literature, who dreams of the splendor of past Roman civilizations. For her, the present is part of a cycle "from which time was to renew his flight, scattering change as he went; and, if her voice or act could mingle aught of good in these changes, this it was to which her imagination most ardently aspired" (*N&SW*, 3:18). Rejecting political factionalism, her vision "darted into futurity, to the hope of freedom for Italy, of revived learning and the reign of peace for all the world: wild dreams, that still awake the minds of men to high song and glorious action" (3:19). Castruccio stands for ruthless power; Euthanasia reflects the Shelleys' cyclical view of history that, as in P. B. Shelley's *Prometheus Unbound,* can bring a new era of social justice despite temporary setbacks.

Valperga weaves the contest between Euthanasia and Castruccio into factual Guelph-Ghibelline political intrigues and historical battles, with the fictitious Castruccio as victorious as the real. And Euthanasia's role as protector of Florentine republicanism may be drawn from the true story of the eleventh-century Countess Matilda (1046–1115), margravine of Tuscany, who retained the loyalty of Florence in its successful defense against the invasion of Emperor Henry IV of Saxony. But in Mary Shelley's version Castruccio's victory over the Florentines is both political and personal: Euthanasia, allied with the Florentines, is conquered; Valperga, Castruccio's own refuge as a child, is destroyed. Euthanasia's act of breaking her engagement to Castruccio illustrates her commitment to the concept of a universal love that supersedes both personal love and social systems based on power. One reviewer of *Valperga* protested that "it scarcely seems in woman's nature for patriotism to be a stronger feeling than love," thus ironically identifying a significant sociopolitical subtext in *Valperga.*[27] Through the delineation of Euthanasia's independence and intellect, the novel resists conventional notions of "woman's nature."

A second fictional character, Beatrice, also resists conventional notions, not through the force of mind demonstrated by Euthanasia but rather through illusory behavior unchecked by reason and education. Beatrice, a religious prophet, is given her own link to actual history through the story of the late twelfth-century Wilhelmina of Bohemia, who with her acolyte Mayfreda (in *Valperga*, Magfreda) formed a secret religious society in Milan.[28] Her believers thought Wilhelmina "was the Holy Ghost incarnate [put] upon earth for the salvation of the female sex" (*N&SW*, 3:130–31). Her role was to replace the male-dominated Catholic religion, which was morally and politically corrupt in that era. But Mary Shelley moves away from historical accuracy when she has Wilhelmina bear Beatrice as the result of what her sect believes to be an immaculate conception.[29] The child, raised by an influential bishop and his widowed sister, rejects their conventional Catholicism and, unaware, takes her mother's path. Like Wilhelmina, Beatrice believes herself elevated by holy grace and becomes a prophet who draws both devoted followers and the wrath of the Catholic Church.

The Inquisition's trial of Beatrice for heresy is thwarted through a conspiracy of sympathetic abbots, who arrange for her to walk across fiery ploughshares, proving that she has survived the "Judgment of God." Those who witness the trial, and Beatrice herself, are further convinced that she is the spiritual child of God, reinforcing the seventeen-year-old Beatrice's delusion that she is invincible. Misled by her elders, as Castruccio was misled in his upbringing, Beatrice survives the religious test only to fail in the secular. In love with Castruccio, she "surrendered herself to his arms" (*N&SW*, 3:151), believing their sexual relationship to be a blessed union. Still engaged to Euthanasia, Castruccio deserts Beatrice, who as a result becomes a deranged beggar. In Beatrice's last days Euthanasia, knowing the truth of Beatrice's story, nevertheless shelters her. In contrast, Castruccio merely eases his conscience by insisting on an elaborate state funeral for the girl he seduced and abandoned.

Later, when Castruccio defeats Euthanasia and the Florentines, he again eases his conscience. Rather than have Euthanasia endure the torture and execution to which he condemns her allies, he exiles her. En route to Sicily her ship is caught in a storm, and Euthanasia drowns with all aboard. Mary Shelley writes of her death, "Earth felt no change when she died; and men forgot her" (3:322), words she echoed about P. B. Shelley in her prefaces to his *Posthumous Poems* and *Poetical Works*.[30]

But neither death was viewed by Mary Shelley as the end of their stories. However tragic, they represented for her transitory reversals in her vision of history as ever advancing, an ideal voiced earlier by Euthanasia. Two years after Euthanasia's death, when Castruccio, though victorious in battle, falls ill and is dying, he himself is assigned by Mary Shelley to repeat this same philosophy, predicting: "Io morro, e vedrete il mondo per varie turbolenze confondersi, e rivoltarsi ogni cosa,"[31] ironically recognizing the very flux Euthanasia relied upon. In fact, shortly after Castruccio's death his personal empire did collapse,[32] signaling that the next cycle had begun.

During the era in which Mary Shelley wrote *Valperga* the United States was the only operative federal democracy;[33] throughout Europe monarchy was again in control. In the concept of historical cycles both Shelleys saw the possibility of reform that could lead the way to enlightened sociopolitical systems. The different yet related characters of the women, resonating with Mary Wollstonecraft's arguments for equal rights for women, are the key to that reform. Beatrice, an unenlightened victim, is led astray as much by religious as by secular deception. Wilhelmina's alternative vision of religious belief iterates the original concepts of Christian benevolence but excludes men. Euthanasia exemplifies both the secular version of Wilhelmina's humanitarian beliefs and its extension to all people. In contrast with Castruccio's actual world, controlled by violence and deceit, Euthanasia symbolizes universal re-creation configured on traits often regarded as feminine—love, peace, charity. Through Euthanasia, Mary Shelley interpolates her English Romantic vision of a world in which love might ultimately defeat power. Inherent in this is the implication that access to political reform lay outside society as it was constructed in medieval times as well as in her own, but not outside the human imagination.

Critics have interpreted in various ways Mary Shelley's 1837 lament that *Valperga* never had "fair play" (see *N&SW*, vol. 3, introductory note). One reason *Valperga* never achieved the popularity that she, P. B. Shelley, and Godwin expected for the novel may well be found in its contemporary reviews. Prior to and during the period in which she wrote this first of two explicitly political novels, Mary Shelley's letters record how focused she was on politics and the cause of reform, referring to herself as a "Joan Bull."[34] Though the reviews were largely positive, they omitted discussion of *Valperga*'s central political focus. Reviewers admired Euthanasia as the epitome of feminine virtue rather than as an unconventional political woman who actively participated in the Florentine faction's war against her tyrant-beloved. Nor did they discuss the reasons why Euthanasia and the religious, ultimately victimized Beatrice were introduced into the story. In short, they do not discuss how Mary Shelley used the invented characters of Euthanasia and Beatrice to lead her readers to the issues of power and values that are the crux of the novel. Mary Shelley may have chosen the unusual name of Euthanasia as a signpost to that meaning. Just as Mary Shelley suggests through this character the return to ancient values, however idealized, perhaps she was suggesting that readers understand the name not in terms of the relatively modern

definition of "gentle" or "good" death (which would belie
her drowning) but according to its literal meaning in
Greek, "noble death."[35]

The fact that *Mrs.* Shelley wrote *Valperga* primed critics to
classify the novel as a love story flawed by too much history.
In ignoring the central theme of the novel and concentrat-
ing instead on the romantic interest, reviewers shifted
Mary Shelley from a sociopolitical Romantic reformer to a
romance writer in the modern sense. During her lifetime
this view became canonical, and it was passed on to twentieth-century readers in a skewed patrimony that insisted
Mary Shelley was either nonpolitical or interested in politics only when P. B. Shelley was alive.[36] But we may only
grasp *Valperga*'s significance if it is recognized to be about
the politics of power contrasted with the power of love, its
open, cyclical ending both an invitation and a challenge
rather than the happy or at least conclusive ending one
might find in a romance.

Mary Shelley's next literary project again reflects the
Shelleys' literary collaboration as well as their shared interest in Latin and Greek literature, mythology, and history.
She wrote the mythological dramas *Proserpine* and *Midas*
(*N&SW*, 2:69–111),[37] for which P. B. Shelley wrote four
lyrics. The dramas appear to be directed towards a younger
audience, which explains why *Proserpine* focuses not on the
rape but instead on the struggle between Ceres and Pluto;
and Midas' tale is given as a "comic drama."[38] But in that
struggle, as well as in the story of Midas's greed, Mary Shel-

ley continued her exploration of power and responsibility, transforming the myths for the consumption of young readers much as Godwin had done in his children's books. Following the dramas, she wrote "Maurice," a "story for Laurette," the Masons' eleven-year-old daughter. Long lost, the thirty-nine-page story, in Mary Shelley's handwriting, has recently been located by descendants of the Masons.[39]

During these years the Shelleys' friends included Byron's lover, Countess Teresa Guiccioli, P. B. Shelley's cousin Thomas Medwin, the adventurer John Trelawny, and Jane and Edward Williams. Despite the disharmony that followed William Shelley's death, the context of their larger circle, most of whom in one way or another lived outside of conventional society, allowed Mary Shelley to lead the intellectual and writer's life so natural to her. The Shelleys moved into Casa Magni at San Terenzo on 30 April; on 4 May the Williamses joined them. P. B. Shelley was much taken at this time with Jane Williams, and Mary Shelley had strong feelings of affection for Edward Williams. The depth of their mutual relationships is unclear. Certainly, Jane Williams appeared to be very much in love with her common-law husband. And the Shelleys were expecting another child, until Mary Shelley suffered a near-fatal miscarriage on 16 June and was saved by P. B. Shelley's insistence that she be placed in a tub of ice to stop the hemorrhaging. Perhaps the Shelleys and the Williamses at this point were experimenting to some degree with P. B. Shel-

ley's doctrine of expansive rather than exclusive love, reflected in his poem *Epipsychidion:*

> I never was attached to that great sect,
> Whose doctrine is, that each one should select
> Out of the crowd a mistress or a friend,
> And all the rest, though fair and wise, commend
> To cold oblivion . . .
>   (lines 149–52)[40]

But the complexities and the relationships came to a tragic
denouement that summer: on 8 July 1822, P. B. Shelley
and Edward Williams drowned in the Bay of Spezia.

Mary Shelley, almost twenty-five, with one surviving
child, Percy Florence, was suddenly cast from having "made
a part of the Elect"[41] into a world she would find inhospitable to both her temperament and her intellect. Her affect-
ing description of the events surrounding the deaths of P.
B. Shelley and Williams gives voice to both the writer and
the widow.[42] She outlines the events, the concerns of their
friends in Leghorn when P. B. Shelley and Williams set
sail, her own and Jane Williams's growing trepidations, and
the recovery and cremation of their bodies: "They are now
about this fearful office—& I live!"[43] She makes no attempt
to imagine P. B. Shelley's and Williams's ordeal, an absence as poignant as the one that would mark the remain-
der of her life. After P. B. Shelley's death, Mary Shelley
and Percy Florence, first accompanied by Jane Williams,
now appropriated as a dear friend, moved to Genoa, where

she lived with the Hunts near Byron and Teresa Guiccioli. Claire Clairmont left to join her brother in Vienna; Jane Williams left for England.

Asserting her independence, with no source of income, Mary Shelley planned to remain on the Continent, hoping that Sir Timothy would be prevailed upon to give some support to his son's widow and grandchild. This she would augment with the income garnered from her own and P. B. Shelley's publications, thus continuing the Shelleys' collaborative professional relationship. Mary Shelley turned to the editing of P. B. Shelley's manuscripts shortly after his death,[44] much as Godwin had turned to Wollstonecraft's. In the same pattern, she also planned to write P. B. Shelley's biography, which she began between February and March 1823 or 1824 but never completed.[45] While still in Italy, sorting out Sir Timothy's demands against her own determination, Mary Shelley prepared for press a number of their works for the *Liberal* (1822 and 1823), the journal that Byron, Leigh Hunt, and P. B. Shelley had intended to publish jointly.[46] Included is Mary Shelley's short story "A Tale of the Passions," two biographical articles, "Madame D'Houtetot" and "Giovanni Villani" (*N&SW*, 2:113), and three works by P. B. Shelley.[47] And in 1823 both *Valperga,* edited by Godwin, and the edition of *Frankenstein* arranged by Godwin (see *N&SW*, vol. 1, introductory note) were published.

These successes in publishing might have allowed her to fulfill her intention to remain on the Continent, but Mary

Shelley was far less successful in her dealings with Sir Timothy Shelley. When his attempt to disprove a legal marriage between the Shelleys failed, he demanded full custody of Percy Florence in exchange for the child's support. On Mary Shelley's refusal, Sir Timothy indicated that he would consider nothing unless Mary Shelley returned with the child to England. In Percy Florence's interest, on 25 August 1823 she complied. She proved, however, to be an energetic adversary. Although her father-in-law refused ever to meet her, Mary Shelley vigorously negotiated with him through his legal representatives to provide the funds necessary to raise her child. In November 1823 she began to receive £100 a year, an allowance that would gradually increase as Percy Florence went from schooling at Slater's in London on to Harrow and to Trinity College, Cambridge, fulfilling the Shelleys' educational aspirations for their son.[48] Though the allowance was actually a loan, repayable on her inheritance at Sir Timothy's death, to obtain each increase to meet the child's expenses demanded exceptional persistence. In her relationship with her father-in-law we see another indicator of a woman who broke the social codes even as she smarted under their existence.

CHAPTER THREE

Return to England, 1823–1837

O N her return to England, despite her recognition as the author of two novels and the celebrity from the first of a seemingly unbroken string of dramatizations of *Frankenstein*,[1] Mary Shelley felt twice exiled. When later she spoke of the difficulties in England for an "unprotected woman,"[2] she was referring to the loss of her primary source of freedom: her husband and the circle of friends who shared their larger values as well as their lives. But she also meant Italy itself, where she had been free of the constraints of both English and Italian social mores. In London, she realized almost at once that a woman who meant to write professionally and live independently would be constantly at odds with an already "Victorianized" English society. Her objective to develop for the iconoclastic P. B. Shelley the large, appreciative readership he had never had in his lifetime added further to this dissonance.

Mary Shelley's next accomplishment towards this end came in June 1824, when she brought out her edition of P. B. Shelley's *Posthumous Poems,* of which five hundred copies were printed. Her preface delineates

her editorial decision to include incomplete poems, translations, and poems out of print, in many instances deci-
phering drafts and putting together "fragments of paper
which in the hands of an indifferent person would never
have been deciphered."[3] To cultivate a new readership for
P. B. Shelley, Mary Shelley decided that this first of her
editions of his works would be "a specimen of how he could
write without shocking any one—and afterwards an edition
of the whole might be got up inserting any thing too shocking for this Vol."[4] In other words, *Posthumous Poems* was a
conscious initial act of public persuasion, much as a
number of the prefaces to their works ambiguously veil the
radicalism of the work itself to draw in a resistant audience.

Still, the volume, published by John and Henry L.
Hunt, was associated with the radical press through John
Hunt (Leigh Hunt's brother and one-time partner), who
in 1824 had just completed a second term in jail for sedi-
tious libel.[5] Nor is the volume as innocent as might appear
at first. Mary Shelley characterizes P. B. Shelley as "an ele-
gant scholar and a profound metaphysician" whose "fearless enthusiasm" for improving "the moral and physical
state of mankind, was the chief reason why he, like other
illustrious reformers, was pursued by hatred and calumny"
(*N&SW,* 2:238). Her comments, though brief, place P. B.
Shelley in historical context and foreshadow her notes and
prefaces to the 1839 editions of his works, making her both
his editor and his collaborator. They also demonstrate her
own political awareness and commitment.

More than three hundred copies of the edition were sold within two months, and the *Posthumous Poems* has been credited with "the steady rise of interest in Shelley's poetry during the following years."[6] Mary Shelley fully expected to publish more of P. B. Shelley's works shortly[7] and to write and publish his biography as well. His father, however, demanded the suppression of the unsold copies and her promise not to publish any more of P. B. Shelley's works during his lifetime as requisite for the repayable allowance for Percy Florence's support. Believing that Sir Timothy's advanced age would not long prevent the publications, she acquiesced, only to wait some fifteen years before she could continue to publish P. B. Shelley's works.[8]

In the meantime, Mary Shelley actively pursued her own writing. Between 1824 and 1839 she published a number of short works.[9] Her stories, appearing in magazines and the newly popular Christmas annuals and occasionally reprinted, were often written to accompany engravings supplied by the publisher.[10] This limitation, a challenge to the creative mind, was superseded by the greater limitation of the publishers' intended audience: these holiday gift books were directed mainly to what was believed proper for women readers. Many of the stories echo the themes of Mary Shelley's novels: family relationships, power, love, religion, the supernatural. Generally, however, the intensity, psychological explorations, complexity of character, and political subtexts of the novels are absent. Instead, the reader is given Mary Shelley's pervasive subjects modified

[69]

in well-honed, noncontroversial expression. Despite the circumstances of composition and audience, in their own terms these stories are accomplished and also reveal her ability, as a professional writer, to produce on call.

Along with the stories, Mary Shelley produced a series of important essays (*N&SW*, vol. 2). They include biographical sketches, book reviews (including one of Godwin's novel *Cloudesley*), and the biographical sketch of Godwin for the 1831 reprint of *Caleb Williams*. Though their purposes vary, most include discussions that reflect Romantic values of imagination, the self transfigured into the universal, the dignity of the individual, and the significance of the writer. In the sketch "Madame D'Houtetot," for example, she comments: "It is the attribute of genius to gift with immortality all the objects it deigns to hallow by its touch" (2:117). In "Giovanni Villani" she cites the current arguments over Classical versus Romantic writers. "Methinks it is both presumptuous and sacrilegious to pretend to give the law to genius" (2:128), using the analogy of the "fixed stars" that "appear to aberrate; but it is we that move, not they" as she argues for receptivity of the unfamiliar. "On Ghosts" speaks of "something beyond us of which we are ignorant . . . thus beyond our soul's ken there is an empty space" in which "influences do exist to watch and guard us, though they be impalpable to the coarser faculties" (2:143), offering a transcendental concept dissociated from traditional Christian religious belief. "The English in Italy" (2:147–63) combines commentary on social and political conditions in Italy and the problem of Austrian oppression (expanded later in *Rambles*) with commentary on good fiction, which "must never divest itself of a certain idealism, which forms its chief beauty" (2:161). "A Visit to Brighton" criticizes the resort as ugly and frivolous, almost surely reflecting her feeling that "every association with the sea is painful: it is a murderer, a remorseless destroyer . . . its strangling waters have stolen life from the young, the wise, the good" (2:170).

Mary Shelley's review of the "Illyrian Poems" gave her the opportunity to praise her friend Prosper Mérimée and at the same time tacitly defend P. B. Shelley, for both selected the topic of incest: "the imaginative writer . . . courageously launches forth, leaving the dull every-day earth behind him" (2:180). Again in "Modern Italy" she includes important democratic political statements along with a definition of those who possess imagination: "Works of art belong to the imagination, certain forms of which they realize; those who do not possess this portion of mind are incapable of perceiving the excellence of the objects created only to be understood by it—their criticisms stand for nothing" (2:186). "Loves of the Poets" explicitly defends P. B. Shelley, his concept of love, and the power of the Poet, "which wakens melody in the silent chords of the human heart" (2:196). Her review of Mérimée's *1572 Chronique du Temps de Charles IX* (2:210–17) is an opportunity for political commentary about "the hollow peace patched up between Charles IX and the admiral de Coligny" (2:210).

Though Blackwood suggested that her review of Godwin's *Cloudesley* (2:201–9) might be "rather a little partial,"[11] she nevertheless offers a telling description of the characteristics of Godwin's style—and even some shortcomings. She praises Cooper's *Bravo* for its handling of "the many forms of the visible universe . . . in their changes of storm or calm" and is grateful that he has not "Italianized himself" but instead demonstrates how his style paints "a picture of social misfortunes and political crimes, which could never have birth under their free government" (*N&SW,* 2:219, 221–22).

Concealed by the anonymity of the articles, Mary Shelley broke Sir Timothy Shelley's injunction to laud P. B. Shelley directly and indirectly. Taken together, the essays form an important statement of contemporary critical observation as well as Romantic philosophy. Whatever the accomplishments of those reviews, however, her own dissatisfaction with the genre of the stories and reviews prompted her to declare to Leigh Hunt, "I write bad articles which help to make me miserable—but I am going to plunge into a novel, and hope that its clear water will wash off the <dirt> mud of the magazines."[12]

That novel, *The Last Man* (1826), brought her the most scathing reviews of any of her works (see *N&SW,* vol. 3, introductory note) fundamentally because readers refused to understand its uses of the imagination as curative or, as with *Valperga,* to accept its larger parable of personal and societal politics.[13] Today, for good reason, *The Last Man* is generally regarded as her second-best novel, and like *Frankenstein,* it continues to elicit a wide variety of interpretations. It has been represented as a rejection of Shelleyan Romanticism and thus of P. B. Shelley himself; as an argument only for the conventional, nuclear family rather than a more comprehensive reformist political vision; as "grief work"; as an exemplar of the obstacles female authors of the era faced; as a *roman à clef;* and as an "apocalyptic vision without determinacy or millennium."[14] While these interpretations reflect aspects of the novel, they are largely selective and often uncritically replicate the reception history of the novel when it was first published.

The political significance of the novel received little notice, no doubt because women were not expected to write about politics. Even more than in the case of her earlier novels, the vitriolic critical reception of *The Last Man* (*N&SW,* vol. 4, introductory note) demonstrates one of the major barriers Mary Shelley encountered in her audiences then— and often now: the failure to accept that her major works are designed to address public and domestic politics. To consider the novel a rejection of Shelleyan Romanticism, to narrow her politics exclusively to women's issues, or to depoliticize her is inconsistent with the abiding philosophy in Mary Shelley's works and precludes the essential Romanticism—and radicalism—of *The Last Man.* This essential Romanticism in theory and philosophy permeates the novel and substantially differentiates this last-man saga from the others of the era at the same time that it constitutes its present modernity (see *N&SW,* vol. 4, introductory note).

Set in the twenty-first century, *The Last Man* tells the story of six characters who belong to the supposedly final generation of humans on earth: the narrator and survivor, Lionel Verney; his sister, Perdita, who marries Lord Raymond, adventurer, hero, nobleman, and eventually head of state; Adrian, earl of Windsor, son of the last king of England (England is at the time a republic governed by an elected lord protector); Adrian's sister, Princess Idris, who defies her mother (the countess of Windsor) and marries Verne; and Evadne, a Greek princess, loved by Adrian, who rejects him in favor of her passion for Raymond, which results in an adulterous affair. As in *Valperga,* the characters' lives are played out in a context in which personal, domestic interests are superseded by political exigencies. But in this case the political exigencies are superseded by an uncontrollable plague that appears to engulf the human species.[15]

In certain aspects the characters bear more than a passing resemblance to members of the Shelley circle—Mary Shelley, P. B. Shelley, Claire Clairmont, and Byron— frequently provoking literal biographical identification. Mary Shelley herself noted that in *The Last Man* could be found "in Lord Raymond and Count Adrian faint portraits . . . of B.[Byron] and S—— but this is a secret."[16]

In a number of important critical commentaries Mary Shelley delineates what she regards as the appropriate role of such "faint portraits" in fiction and poetry. In "Giovanni Villani" she endorses the Romantic model of the author's "intrusion of self in a work of art," arguing that the "habit of self-analysation and display" results in books in which "the human heart" is like "the undiscovered country." This leads to works that are the favorites among men "of imagination and sensibility" (*N&SW*, 2:129–30). Continuing her setting of standards for both authors and readers in "Modern Italy" (see above), she adds a third, telling caution about autobiographical writing in her review of Godwin's novel *Cloudesley*: "The merely copying from our own hearts will no more form a first-rate work of art, than will the most exquisite representation of mountains, water, wood, and glorious clouds, form a good painting, if none of the rules of grouping or colouring are followed" (2:203).

Other critics in the period also attempted to resolve the problem of incorporating the self into literature and its transfiguration into impersonal forms. Samuel Taylor Coleridge recognized this conflict as the secondary imagination's struggle "to idealize and to unify," and William Hazlitt summarized the same concept by the term "keeping." The criterion for P. B. Shelley was "the creation of actions according to the unchangeable forms of human nature, as existing in the mind of the creator, which is itself the image of all other minds."[17] Mary Shelley, in the *Cloudesley* review, perhaps echoing Hazlitt, also uses "keeping" to sum up what she regarded as this essential objectification and coherence of art.

Reflecting Mary Shelley's own theories, the characters in *The Last Man* demonstrate reformulated attributes, shaped in accord with her goal not of biography but of Romantic dislocation. The dislocation begins with the novel's introduction, in which an unnamed narrator and companion discover the leaves of a manuscript in the cave of the Cumaean Sibyl, a prophet of classical legend whose last three volumes of oracular utterances are said to have been destroyed by fire in 83 B.C. This remarkable find takes place in the era in which the novel is written. The events depicted in the leaves, written in many languages, are predicted to occur two centuries after the story is told. Thus, the reader is subjected to an unequivocal belief in the Sibyl; the juggle of time, in which flying balloons for transportation are counterpoised with an ongoing Greek war for independence; a prophecy, to be disbelieved at peril, emanating from a religion prior to, and in conflict with, Christianity; and equally dislocating, the nonidentity of the first-person author and the companion in the introduction.

The Shelleys actually did visit the Sibyl's cave in 1818.[18] The conflation of this visit with the narrator's allows Mary Shelley to intensify the indeterminacy that is at the heart of the novel, in which the actual author is also associated by indirection as a result of Sir Timothy Shelley's prohibition

[76]

against bringing forward the Shelley name. (In fact, after a review of *The Last Man*, "by the Author of Frankenstein," mentioned her name, Sir Timothy temporarily withheld the allowance.) In short, the reader is positioned in a cave of insecurities, requiring a torch to find the path and uncertain, at best, of what will be found at the end of a dangerous, uncomfortable journey. That journey, like Mathilda's narrative, encompasses the very act of writing itself. This telling, again like the earlier one after the deaths of Clara and William, extends far beyond the subjective. In a transposition of the word as holy, the words of the novel trace the gradual, Job-like education of the imagination of its narrator, Lionel Verney, from aggressive narcissism to a transforming human understanding that enlarges the imagination beyond ordinary limitations and opens new possibilities both to its readers and to its author.

The roles of women and men are consciously displaced throughout *The Last Man,* beginning with the ungendered narrator and the ungendered companion. Verney often comments on female versus male responses to emotional experiences, self-consciously fearful of being "girlish" but, in the end, gratefully responding with ardent emotion (*N&SW,* 4:314) and tears (4:345), thereby blurring the typical boundaries between female and male. The countess of Windsor is depicted as tyrannical and unprincipled, traits traditionally associated with men. Evadne's warrior role is acted out in male disguise, and there is also a string of vignettes about other young women heroically undaunted in the face of deprivation and death as well as a band of female religious fanatics "more eager and resolute than their male companions" to engage in battle (4:296). *The Last Man* presents a radical vision of a world that does not reject men or women per se but rather rejects the restrictions imposed on their personal and societal roles.[19] A further destabilization occurs in Verney's hope, expressed towards the conclusion, for the existence of a brother and sister, the "children of a saved pair of lovers" (*N&SW,* 4:362), who would survive to repeople the earth. Both a triumphant Laon and Cythna and an awakened Victor Frankenstein and Elizabeth Lavenza are suggested in Mary Shelley's parody of Adam and Eve, which functions as an irreverent reminder of the incestuous beginnings of humanity in the Judeo-Christian tradition and thereby an irreverent parody on the tradition itself.

Reviewers of the era resisted the politics and religion of *The Last Man* at the same time that they excoriated its graphic descriptions (see *N&SW,* vol. 4, introductory note) and flights of imagination. In a post-Napoleonic age when conservative Europe restored monarchs to thrones, when a middle class wanted its share of power within a newly establishing order that it wished to control, and when the middle and upper classes in England were frightened by working-class uprisings, the model of a republican government replacing the monarchy was even in theory sharply disruptive to the status quo. Furthermore, *The Last Man* suggests that republican government could also prove to be inadequate in the context of an endemic failure of its parliamentarians who are enthralled by their own politics of power.[20] England is presented as politically insular, symbolized by its national credo that its island shores will protect it from the plague that is devastating the rest of the world. Conspicuously absent in this isolationist republicanism is the system of universal education advocated by the Shelleys, Godwin, and Wollstonecraft. Consequently, nothing prepares the populace for either republican governance and responsibility at home or genuine engagement and concern with world politics.

The Last Man is also aligned with Shelleyan, Godwinian, and Wollstonecraftian politics in its efforts to alter ordinary perspectives. It dismantles expected values—genuine love of wife and children, traditional religion, and traditional government—in order to compel readers to reconsider and reconstruct those values, to, by analogy, envision a world-view that above all else permits possibility. This dismantling encompasses the deaths of Verney's loved ones. His family intact, Verney would have remained locked in a nuclear family, just as without expanded perspectives the world would be locked in self-interest and fail to achieve a larger concern for society as a whole. The loss does not suggest that Mary Shelley was rationalizing the deaths of P. B. Shelley and her children in the name of that greater good, as had Godwin in his hypothetical story of the need to rescue Bishop Fénélon from a fire at the cost of leaving one's mother (later changed to servant) to perish.[21]

Such biographical assumptions disregard the fact that *The Last Man,* in its science, in its slippery time and place, in its complexities of female-male relationships, and in its politics, is consciously premised as fable.

Mary Shelley's use of the fable is not accidental but rather an immediate outcome of the education she received from Godwin's theory of inspiring children's imaginations. In *Frankenstein* Mary Shelley reflected not only the sociopolitical issues of Godwin's *Caleb Williams* but the chase-and-flight structure of the book as well. It is reasonable to speculate that her father's own love of fairy-tales, the children's tales he and Mary Jane Godwin wrote,[22] and the other early works of imagination to which she was exposed provided her with another model through which to articulate the egalitarian philosophy she shared with her parents and her husband.

The Last Man is an adult fairy tale of ghastly deaths by plague, graphic battle scenes, and impassioned love in which Mary Shelley reinvents what she lamented as absent from much literature of the day. In "On Ghosts" she defines that absence as the "empire of the imagination" that permitted enchantresses, "dungeons of palpable darkness," "fairies and their wands," "witches and their familiars," and "ghosts, with beckoning hands and fleeting shapes" of a "wiser age" (*N&SW*, 2:141). More dire than anything found in the tales of the *Arabian Nights,* which she cites, or Grimm or Aesop, *The Last Man* carries with it a most complex and challenging lesson to be learned. When Verney

calls on his reader, "whoever thou art, wherever thou dwel-
lest, whether of race spiritual, or, sprung from some surviving pair" to "here read of the acts of the extinct race"
and "learn the deeds and sufferings of thy predecessors"
(4:310), readers are encouraged to question their own
identities as well as their origins and their destinies.

Mary Shelley almost certainly drew on other mythic
models to construct a world that seems to be destroyed but
is not. One was P. B. Shelley's poem *The Sensitive Plant,* a representation of the belief that existence is never concluded,
despite the wintry disappearance of the flowers.[23] Another,
the biblical tale of the peopling of the earth from Ararat as
a "mere plaything of nature, when first it crept out of uncreative void into light; but thought brought forth power
and knowledge; and clad with these, the race of man assumed dignity and authority" (*N&SW,* 4:319). When Verney
cries out that "the game is up! We must all die; nor leave
survivor nor heir to the wide inheritance of earth" (4:320)
he draws on that first peopling "out of uncreative void" to
himself disaffirm that extinction: "Surely death is not
death, and humanity is not extinct; but merely passed into
other shapes, unsubjected to our perceptions" (4:320).
Thus Verney becomes a seer, like the Sibyl, his cave the
cave of the world; the Sibyl's leaves found in the introduction become Verney's, and by extension the seer is also
Mary Shelley.

This reaffirmation, as well as the other affirmations in
the closing pages of the novel, which each time counter

Verney's despair, are apropos only within a context that enfranchises a new world order and a new world understanding. In Verney's decision to sail to Rome, "sovereign mistress of the imagination, majestic and eternal survivor of millions of generations of extinct men" (4:357), Mary Shelley offers another meaning not only to the notion of extinction but also to what she regards as the life force of existence itself: the imagination. A critic recently posited that *The Last Man* by 1826 had become "ridiculous" rather than apocalyptic in light of the plethora of last-man poems and books but added that "behind the ridicule . . . there is a suggestion that the imagination resists the idea of Lastness, an idea that presupposes a recipient or reader whose very existence negates the Lastness of the narrating subject."[24] This resistance of lastness, or the idea the imagination resists anything, was precisely one of the notions Mary Shelley's works contested in their effort to extend the structures of human experience.

The first-person narrator of the introduction speaks of writing as taking the narrator "out of a world, which has averted its once benignant face from me, to one glowing with imagination and power . . . such is human nature, that the excitement of mind was dear to me, and the imagination, painter of tempest and earthquake, or, worse, the stormy and ruin-fraught passions of man, softened my real sorrows and endless regrets, by clothing these fictitious ones in that ideality, which takes the mortal sting from pain" (*N&SW*, 4:8–9). Thus, the narrator and Verney share the same redemptive experience: through writing, through imagination, they reshape their sorrows into an "ideality." This is Mary Shelley in the process of what Fiona Stafford has called "grief work," as when she wrote *Matilda* and found that "the inspiration was sufficient to quell my wretchedness temporarily."[25] But it is not an ordinary mourning process. Rather, it is Mary Shelley who even in mourning indicates her belief that her destiny was to write.[26] After P. B. Shelley's death, she expressed confidence in her ability to maintain herself and Percy Florence through writing.[27] Repeatedly, in letters and journals, she spoke of imagination as the fulcrum of her life and struggled to sustain that imagination, which she relied on from her early childhood to the end of her life, intent on finding compelling modes of expression for her own special way of seeing.

One journal entry is much cited by critics in reference to *The Last Man:* "The *Last Man!* Yes I may well describe that solitary being's feelings, feeling myself as the last relic of a beloved race, my companions extinct before me."[28] But this reflection must be situated within a fundamental doctrine expressed in another journal entry, a doctrine that resonates in Mary Shelley's works throughout her life, and in which she found enduring strength: "What should I have done if my Imagination had not been my companion?"[29] She, like P. B. Shelley, used imagination as agent.[30]

Rather than deny P. B. Shelley's and her parents' political ideologies, in *The Last Man* Mary Shelley continues to voice them as survivor, as does Verney. Its biographical re-verberation is not in simple *roman à clef* but in her assertion of the importance of the imagination. *The Last Man* has further biographical resonance. For all her recognition of loss, and in spite of equivocal feelings at times, the novel is another example of Mary Shelley's extraordinary creativity and assertiveness, which prevailed in her writing, her continual battles with Sir Timothy about support for Percy Florence, and the shaping of her own life.

When Mary Shelley returned to England in 1823, she found herself in an "island-prison"[31] that was quickly solidifying around a materialistic value system in which women's lives were increasingly restricted. The sociopolitical agenda in the fiction of *The Last Man* left open possibilities that appeared to be closing in reality. It was disturbing because its vision underscored the need for a different kind of meta-story, one that could be subscribed to by an egalitarian, educated world rather than one that seemed merely to shift the pockets of wealth and power from the aristocracy to the industrialists. The world of the novel advocates daring imagination, which her critics sorely lacked, and which prevented them from joining Verney at the end, when he sets out with "Neither hope nor joy" as his pilots. Instead, he is led on by "restless despair and fierce desire of change" but still expecting to "read fair augury in the rainbow—menace in the cloud—some lesson or record dear to my heart in everything" (*N&SW,* 4:365) as he goes in search, because "it was still possible, that, could I visit the whole extent of earth, I should find in some part of the wide extent a survivor" (4:363).

In *Frankenstein* Mary Shelley constructed a being from parts to startle the world from its complacency. In *The Last Man* she again constructs from parts, this time from the written word. In both novels her purpose was the same. In the anxiety-driven story of *The Last Man,* she associates herself with the visions of the Sibyl, who was the "advisor" of political leaders, as well as with the visions of P. B. Shelley and her parents. Her journal entry of 23 April 1830 sheds particular light on her fusion of imagination and anxiety:

> In a situation like mine, however energetically one helps oneself, one is subject to frequent set-backs, and all these brief respites that one procures for oneself are very precarious. The soul only enjoys them in passing and knows well that it can reach serenity only through a trick of the imagination which it should maintain but which constrains it too much, so that it always comes back to the state it finds more suitable, a state of agitation.

The reviewer who sarcastically caviled that the story should have been about the "Last Woman" would have been far more perceptive to realize what I believe Mary Shelley herself knew full well: her last man reflects the fears and hopes of the last Romantic, who, like Verney, was setting out in search of other survivors. The irony may well be that the most futuristic aspect of *The Last Man* was less its vision of technology than its predicting the issues that continue to face humanity as we enter the twenty-first century.

Mary Shelley's sense of being the last Romantic was reinforced by two events that followed the publication of the novel. In 1826 Charles Shelley died, making Percy Florence heir to the baronetcy. This changed his relationship to his grandfather but left hers unaltered. Then in 1827 Mary Shelley was devastated when she discovered that her beloved friend Jane Williams, who had become the common-law wife of Thomas Jefferson Hogg, had been telling insidious tales about Mary Shelley's relationship with P. B. Shelley to mutual friends.[32] This rupture, not permanent but never fully healed, signified the ending of Mary Shelley's closest link, besides her son, to her years with P. B. Shelley. As a result, she suffered feelings akin to mourning and turned in new directions in pursuit of friendship and community.

Her early daring in rebelling against her father's wishes and eloping with P. B. Shelley was resourcefully activated. In an 1826—28 charade that broke some of the most established beliefs of her society, Mary Shelley risked scandal and thereby the loss of her child when she assisted two of her friends, Mary Diana Dods and Isabella Robinson, in an intercontinental trans-gender charade. Together, the three arranged for Dods and Robinson, passing as Mr. and Mrs. Walter Sholto Douglas, to enter successfully into an elite Anglo-French society in Paris that included General

Lafayette and Prosper Mérimée, a deception undetected until recently.[33] Another example of that daring was her assistance, in 1829, in the publication of P. B. Shelley's works by Galignani, secretly defying Sir Timothy's injunction that the Shelley name not be brought before the public. Unquestionably, Mary Shelley indicated in her journals and letters that she wished to be acknowledged and accepted in society. But these, and other actions, as well as the themes that pervaded her novels, make clear that she, like P. B. Shelley, though forced at times to compromise in the interest of partial victories,[34] wanted this acceptance on her own terms.

Mary Shelley again asserted those terms in *Perkin Warbeck*, her second historical novel.[35] Returning explicitly to the political arena of *Valperga*, she brings the issues of power closer to home in a version of the fifteenth-century historical events surrounding the claim to the English throne. Here, as in her prefaces to *Valperga*[36] and *The Last Man*, Mary Shelley destabilizes expectation. Though the novel demonstrates wide historical research, she denies that a narrative "confined to the incorporation of facts" could "do justice" to the story. More significantly, contrary to most historical accounts, she chooses to premise that a man named Perkin Warbeck was actually, as he claimed, Richard, duke of York, who had survived the Tower and returned, supported by Yorkist allies, to wrest the crown from Henry VII (*N&SW*, vol. 5, preface). In Mary Shelley's scenario, Henry is presented as ruthless and manipulative,

Richard as seemingly idealistic and caring. In the wake of their opposition, however, the mass of society suffers atrocities, deprivations, and death.[37]

At several points Richard perceives the horrors of the war he has actuated and appears to renounce his quest but instead continues to press his claims. Clouded by the standards of a chivalric sociopolitical code, Richard's naive heroic stance is no less destructive than Henry's calculated one. In citing Coleridge's poem, "Fire, Famine, and Slaughter: A War Eclogue" (*N&SW*, 5:120), Mary Shelley speaks to the horrors of war. Another Coleridge poem, "Ode to France," equally well known to her, deals specifically with the same paradox of war as the agent of social justice and anticipates Mary Shelley's own conclusions.[38] In *Prometheus Unbound* P. B. Shelley resolved the problem by having Prometheus renounce his curse on Jupiter, thus freeing himself from the power struggle. In the end, *Perkin Warbeck* centers on the values of a feudal society, with two (and at times, more) opposing kings waging war for power and dominance in the name of honor and hereditary rights and fundamentally indifferent to the interests and welfare of society at large.

Richard is ultimately captured and executed; Henry retains his crown. But Godwin's reformist question resonates from their clash: "What rational man could possibly have given himself the least disturbance for the sake of choosing whether Henry the sixth or Edward the fourth should have the style of king of England?"[39] In treating Richard as the legitimate heir, Mary Shelley echoes Godwin in her attack on the very concept of legitimate monarchical power, as she did in her letters[40] and later again in *Rambles*.

In *Valperga* Mary Shelley introduced the fictional characters Euthanasia and Beatrice, the one to impart republican ideals to the story, the other to function as victim of the political and religious establishment. In *Perkin Warbeck* Mary Shelley fictionalizes her anti-power idealism in the voice of Katherine Gordon (who actually was Richard's wife) and fictionalizes her picture of victim to belief in the power-based system and her own blind love for Richard in Monina de Faro.[41] In this telling, Katherine supports Richard's fight for the crown but perceives both the futility of the attempt as well as the ordeal of ruling that success would bring. She recognizes "a vain mask in all the common-place pomp of palaces; she perceived that power failed most, when its end was good; she saw that in accomplishing its purpose in the cottage, or in halls of state, felicity resulted from the affections only" (*N&SW*, 5:291). Though she does not offer Euthanasia's republican ideals, she asserts that social good cannot be achieved in a power-based system. Rather than conveying an alternative macrocosmic political system, Katherine urges Richard to abandon his public role, rejecting the monarchical system in favor of a moral paradigm based on personal domestic love.

Katherine Gordon's convictions in her concluding monologue have been interpreted as an abandonment by

Mary Shelley of her reformist ideals. But Katherine's beliefs and actions present a version of Promethean renunciation of power on a human scale and its replacement by human empathy for pain and joy: "The more entirely we mingle our emotions with those of others, making our well or ill being depend on theirs, the more completely do we cast away selfishness, and approach the perfection of our nature" (*N&SW*, 5:398). In her need to "love and be loved" and to alleviate the suffering of others (5:400) Katherine Gordon exemplifies a microcosmic conduit to sociopolitical reform as subversive as, but arguably more idealized than, Euthanasia's republicanism. Mary Shelley's sorrow at P. B. Shelley's death resonates in Katherine Gordon's apologia, but Katherine's sphere remains personal within the established system, whereas Mary Shelley continued, in her own writing and in her editing of P. B. Shelley's works, to actively promote reform.

The contemporaneity of the political issues *Perkin Warbeck* raised in monarchical Europe was ignored by its critics. Instead, the reviews can be summed up as treating the book as a romance that showed the "stamp of a powerful mind" and Mary Shelley as an "authoress" who "need not fear comparison to the most talented of her sex."[42] This depoliticizing markedly contrasts with a number of Mary Shelley's highly political letters, written the same year that *Perkin Warbeck* was published, celebrating the 1830 revolution in France. To General Lafayette she sent congratulations, hoping that "every heart in Europe respond . . . bidding the world be free. . . . May England imitate your France in its moderation and heroism. There is great hope that any change among us, will originate with the Government . . . but our position is critical and dreadful—for what course of measures can annihilate the debt? and so reduce the taxation, which corrodes the very vitals of the suffering population of this country."[43] To Trelawny she wrote: "The burnings—the alarms—the absorbing politics of the day . . . God knows how it will all end, but it looks as if the Autocrats would have the good sense to make the necessary sacrifices to a starving people."[44] And in a letter to her friend Robert Dale Owen she celebrates "the triumph of the Cause in Europe" and "a degree of tyrant quellingtiveness,"[45] sentiments she echoes to the reformer Fanny Wright, asking, "Will not our Children live to see a new birth for the world!"[46]

Mary Shelley's next novel, *Lodore* (1835), extends her microcosmic exploration of power and responsibility broached in the values of Katherine Gordon in *Perkin Warbeck*. Unlike the supernatural or historical settings of the earlier novels, *Lodore* is a contemporary novel centered on parent-child relationships and class mores, through which each major character and a number of secondary characters are examined. The pivotal story concerns the self-centered Lodore, the equally self-centered Cornelia, Lady Lodore, and their daughter Ethel. Woven into their story are other parent-child relationships, including those between Lady Santerre and her daughter, Cornelia; Fanny Derham and her parents, Francis Derham and Mrs. Derham; Lodore, his sister Elizabeth Fitzhenry, and their father; Lodore, the Countess Lyzinski, and their illegitimate son, Count Casimir; and Edward Villiers and his father, Colonel Villiers.

The key figures are all members of, or related to, the aristocracy. But this is no silver-fork novel, the genre then gaining popularity. Rather, *Lodore* is the silver fork transformed through a Romantic's vision. The opening epigraph and chapter make clear the connection between the larger political issues and the outcomes of familial and societal politics. *Lodore* dissects aristocratic values to demonstrate that ultimately they are deleterious both personally and societally. In their stead the novel proposes egalitarian educational paradigms for women and men, which would bring social justice as well as the spiritual and intellectual means by which to meet the challenges life invariably brings.

Lodore, in a number of ways, may be seen as a modification and an expansion of the themes of *Matilda.* Lodore's life, like that of Mathilda's unnamed father, is privileged and self-centered. After the end of his adulterous relationship with Countess Lyzinski he attempts to enter the political arena but fails due to his egotism. Running from this disappointment, he seeks escape in nature and isolation but soon finds himself bored. A courtship, in which the thirty-four-year-old Lodore is both manipulator and manipulated, results in his marriage to the sixteen-year-old Cornelia Santerre, a "lovely girl somewhat ignorant" but

"white paper to be written upon at will" (*N&SW,* 6:41).
Trained by her mother, Lady Santerre, to value wealth and
social standing, Cornelia resists Lodore's attempts to control her. Ethel, born to the pair within a year of their marriage, serves only to drive the couple further apart: Lodore
idolizes their daughter, while Cornelia basically ignores
her. Countess Lyzinski and Count Casimir, who is unaware
that Lodore is his father, enter Lodore's set. Casimir's attentions to Cornelia result in Lodore's striking Casimir.
In order not to duel with his own son, Lodore abruptly
leaves for the Continent, appearing to be a coward. After
attempts to convince Cornelia to accompany him miscarry,
he emigrates to Illinois, taking the two-year-old Ethel.

In Illinois, Lodore isolates himself from the community
and molds Ethel into his idea of a model woman, with
problematic results. She benefits because "a daughter,
brought up by a father only" develops early those "portions
of mind" that "under mere feminine tuition" are "often
destroyed" (*N&SW,* 6:15). But Lodore's "incessant care"
made Ethel's spirit "ductile and dependent" (6:15). The
price of Lodore's goal to "educate his daughter to all the
perfection of which the feminine character is susceptible"
was to keep her "pliant to his will" (6:18). Ethel "inspired
her father with more than a father's fondness. He lived but
for and in her" (6:19). Foreshadowing the problems of
such an upbringing, the narrator declares: "A lofty sense of
independence is, in man, the best privilege of his nature.
It cannot be doubted, but that it were for the happiness of

the other sex that she were taught more to rely on and act for herself." Instead, Ethel "was taught to know herself dependent," and as a result, "[s]he seldom thought, and never acted, for herself" (6:19). When Ethel is sixteen, and becomes the object of an inappropriate suitor, Lodore decides they must return to London to provide her with proper society. In New York, Edward Villiers, a young man of good character but inferior education, and Fanny Derham, the ideal of education, come into the Lodore circle while they all await passage to England. When the story of Lodore's "cowardice" over the Casimir incident is scornfully recounted by a man who had been there, Lodore challenges his detractor to a duel. With Villiers as his second, Lodore dies and Ethel becomes the ward of her Aunt Elizabeth in Essex. Initially, like Mathilda, she thinks life will "be one long memory" (6:95), but Ethel, far less victimized than Mathilda by her earlier life, is able to recover.

By the end of the first volume, the title character, who remained constant—victim and victimizer of a bankrupt social system—disappears except in effect and through the memory of the others. The focus shifts to Ethel, handicapped by her dependency but idealistic; and Cornelia, Lady Lodore, who by the story's conclusion finds spiritual renewal through her renunciation of wealth to aid her daughter. Both women are contrasted, overtly and covertly, with Fanny Derham, intellectual, learned, and independent, though poor.

In the ensuing volumes Ethel and Edward fall in love

and marry, their incidents of impoverishment drawn par-
tially from the Shelleys' own experiences (see *N&SW*, vol. 6,
introductory note). Through the legal entanglements that
impact the couple's lives, Mary Shelley voices one of her
consistent themes: the failure of the judicial system. Lodore neglects to rewrite a twelve-year-old will, which leaves
his beloved daughter financially dependent on her aunt;
Colonel Villiers's intrigues lead his son Edward to penury
and jail. When Lady Lodore, estranged from Ethel through
misunderstandings on all parts, decides to cede her wealth
entirely to Ethel, even that noble gesture is temporarily
thwarted by legal machinations. The happy conclusion of
Lodore reminds one somewhat of the conclusion of Brecht's
Threepenny Opera, with its ironic "happy ending." In the
course of events the idealistic Ethel, reconciled with her
mother and now a mother herself, is "always happy" pursuing "a tranquil course" (*N&SW*, 6:312). Lodore's life is ac-
counted as not "fruitless" because of the "care and admira-
ble education he had bestowed on Ethel" (6:312), though
the narrative makes amply clear the shortcomings of that
education and that Ethel's idealism has never been tested
by real want. Cornelia, who "wonders at her past life,"
marries the intellectual and benevolent Horatio Saville;
and Edward Villiers "learnt to prize worldly prosperity at
its true value" (6:312). Consonant with the reformist-ed-
ucation subtext of *Lodore*, the book shifts from the fairy-tale
lives of its principal players to conclude with the fate of
Fanny Derham, the secondary figure who represents the

model, not easily attained, of what a woman—or a man—
should be. Independent, she will "pursue her way un-
flinching; and, in her lofty idea of the dignity of her nature, in her love of truth and in her integrity, she will find
support and reward in her various fortunes . . . by an un-
deviating observance of those moral laws on which all human excellence is founded—a love of truth in ourselves,
and a sincere sympathy with our fellow-creatures" (6:313).

As in *Frankenstein, Valperga, Perkin Warbeck,* and, later, *Falkner,*
the central character of this story is an anti-hero. One may
include in this catalogue Mathilda, who was unable, in
consequence of her upbringing, to get beyond the limitations of her own and her father's culture. The only excep-
tion to this list of anti-heroes is Lionel Verney, the "Last
Man," whose definitive acts of imagination include his incorporation of characteristics generally assigned to women.
In his ability to weep he could be a model for Lodore, who
is unable to incorporate "those habits of effeminacy" that
sometimes prevent young aristocracy "from rebelling
against the restraints of society" (*N&SW,* 6:30) or to be like
his Eton friend, Derham, "slender," "effeminate," "gentle," who had "wild fancies, and strange inexplicable ideas"
but mastered "the abstrusest philosophy" (6:31). Lodore,
for Mary Shelley, was a "type": "The new Lord Lodore was
one of those men, not unfrequently met with in the world,
whose early youth is replete with mighty promise; who, as
they advance in life, continue to excite the expectation, the
curiosity, and even the enthusiasm of all around them; but

as the sun on a stormy day now and then glimmers forth, giving us hopes of conquering brightness, and yet slips down to its evening eclipse without redeeming the pledge" (6:35). In *Lodore* it is not the man who incorporates feminine characteristics to temper and sensitize the spirit but, as if they stepped from the pages of *A Vindication,* two young women—Ethel and Fanny—who exemplify, to different degrees, characteristics generally associated with men in that era: courage, dedication, and intellectual accomplishment.

Mary Shelley does not abandon her reformist views in *Lodore;* she repositions them to comment on the society around her. In the contemporary setting of the novel, home becomes the paradigm for the state. The lives of its inhabitants are conditioned by familial and social education that conduct the individual either to a world of benevolence and mutual care or to one of conflict and mutual destruction. From the many ways of perceiving, "the chief task of the philosopher is to purify and correct the intellectual prism" (*N&SW,* 6:62). Language, the tool of the philosopher, is Mary Shelley's as well: "Words have more power than any one can guess; it is by words that the world's great fight, now in these civilized times, is carried on" (6:213).

In Mary Shelley's last novel, *Falkner,* the female as the model of courage, dedication, and intellectual accomplishment takes center stage. Again set in contemporary England, the principal story concerns Elizabeth Raby, orphaned at the age of six, and Falkner, who is "outwardly unemployed and tranquil; inwardly torn by throes of the most tempestuous and agonizing feelings" (*N&SW*, 7:16-17). Shortly before the story opens, John Rupert Falkner has abducted Alithea Neville, meaning to persuade her to elope with him.[47] Though unhappily married and in love with Falkner from youth, she refuses to leave her son, Gerard Neville, whose last sight of his mother was of her being carried away. Trying to escape from Falkner, she drowns and is secretly buried by the remorseful Falkner and the man who assists him. Not knowing the truth of the episode, Alithea's husband, Sir Boyville, attributes her disappearance to her willing elopement with Falkner and takes out his anger on their son, the constant reminder of his assumed abandonment.

The two main figures first meet in a country churchyard, recalling Mary Shelley's own visits to the St. Pancras grave of her mother. Falkner attempts to commit suicide but is saved by the outcry of the child, whom he befriends and then adopts. In their life together, one of continual travel, Falkner provides Elizabeth with love and care, which she returns to her ever-agonized and guilt-ridden stepfather. Throughout her childhood, Falkner grooms Elizabeth Raby to be as dependent on him as Ethel is on Lodore: "Falkner felt a half remorse at the too great pleasure he derived from her society; while hers was a sort of rapturous, thrilling adoration that dreamt not of the necessity of a check, and luxuriated in its boundless excess" (*N&SW*, 7:35). Elizabeth's education, conducted by both Falkner and Miss Jervis (a governess hired when Elizabeth is ten), schools her in history and biography. "Nor were these more masculine studies" her only lessons; she also learns needlework and "habits of neatness and order" (7:40).

Falkner and Elizabeth Raby's idyllic life comes to a first close when she is about thirteen and meets the sixteen-year-old Gerard Neville, handsome but savage. Faced with the young Neville, Falkner talks again of suicide. Instead, with Elizabeth, he goes off to the Aeonian Isles, then leaves to fight for Greece in its war with Turkey while she remains safely behind. From her thirteenth to her sixteenth year Elizabeth studies philosophy, religion, and music and learns to ride. Mostly alone, her life is "rife with busy visions" that seem almost real (7:56).

In the next phase of their life together the roles of the now educated Elizabeth Raby and Falkner subtly change. It is she who rescues him from the war zone when he is wounded. It is she who evinces a "reliance on her own powers and a forgetfulness of every triviality which haunts the petty minded" (7:68). Elizabeth Raby regulates not only her own "inner spirit" but Falkner's life as well. Never prying into his secret, she determines to reconcile him to life, because "every person whose mind soars above the vulgar, has some exalted and disinterested object in view to which they are ready to sacrifice the common blessings of life" (7:55).

Elizabeth Raby's determination to care for her adopted "Papa," however, does not preclude falling in love with

[99]

Gerard Neville. Later, Neville extends her education, which already includes Shakespeare and Milton, music and German, introducing her to the works of Chaucer, Spenser, Pope, Gray, Burns, and the "writings of a younger, but divine race of poets" (7:223). Nevertheless, she places her filial affection for Falkner before her love for Gerard Neville.

Through Elizabeth Raby, the novel focuses on working out personal affections against the challenge of erroneous beliefs, appearances, and the meaning of justice. When Falkner is brought to trial, she determines, whatever the history or consequences of Alithea Neville's death, to console and support her adopted father. Though considered the "child of a murderer" (7:220), she breaks social codes to be with Falkner, refusing to become a "timid, home-bred young lady, tied by the most frivolous rules, impeded by fictitious notions of propriety and false delicacy . . . whether indeed such submission to society—such useless, degrading dereliction of nobler duties, was adapted for feminine conduct, and whether she, despising such bonds, sought a bold and dangerous freedom, she could not tell; she only knew and felt . . . educated as she had been, beyond the narrow paling of boarding-school ideas, or the refinements of a lady's boudoir" (7:234).

In the course of the trial, Gerard Neville, who echoes P. B. Shelley's *Prometheus* in "hating that the meanest thing that breathed should endure pain" (7:260), accepts Falkner's story of his mother's accidental death. In the end,

Falkner, who in jail "might have served as a model for Prometheus—the vulture at his heart producing pangs and spasms . . . but his will unconquered—his mind refusing to acknowledge the bondage to which his body was the prey" (7:243), is found innocent of the charge of murder. Gerard Neville renounces his oath of vengeance in true Godwinian fashion; the young couple are married; and Elizabeth prevents Falkner from self-exile, insisting instead that he remain a loving part of their family circle.

The John Falkner–Elizabeth Raby relationship revisits the guilty father–innocent daughter relationship in *Matilda* and again poses the recurrent Romantic conflict between self-interest and social need. It is a world in which the good mother (and in Elizabeth Raby's case the good father as well) dies; and those surviving retain a marked affinity with the dead. Just as Falkner sought to have power over Alithea, so he initially seeks power over Elizabeth. The problem of parental power is further contextualized by the control of the wealthy Raby family over their children. Falkner may also be likened to Frankenstein, Castruccio, and Warbeck in his attempt to order the world, but in this story, as with the unnamed father in *Matilda,* the uses and abuses of authority are on a human rather than a supernatural or historical scale.

As in *Lodore,* the personal tribulations in *Falkner* are played out in an environment of societal power, exemplified by the class system as well as by the legal system. The privileges of wealth and class are made obvious. Even Gerard Neville, who from childhood dreams only of clearing his mother's name, argues that Falkner is a gentleman and that a gentleman could never perpetrate the crime of which he is accused. Though she believes Falkner innocent, Elizabeth Raby instead offers a Godwinian rationale for Falkner's actions: "[E]ven where guilt is joined to the hardness of habitual vice . . . it ought to be treated with the indulgence of a correcting father, not by the cruel vengeance of the law" (7:237). Class and religion also come into play in the story of Elizabeth Raby's paternal family. The oldest family in England and extremely wealthy, the Rabys are outside the establishment because they are Catholic. When Edwin Raby gives up his faith to marry, the Rabys exercise their power and disown him; and though Elizabeth impresses them most favorably, initially they cannot discard their prejudices.

Most reviewers regarded *Falkner* as a romance, though noting some parallels with Godwin's novels. Clearly, Falkner's acquittal and acceptance works out Godwin's concept of personal reconstruction rather than the legal vengeance portrayed at the conclusion of *Caleb*. But this novel, like Mary Shelley's other post-*Frankenstein* novels, goes beyond Godwinian exploration to Romantic resolution in its demonstration of ways of taking responsibility and ways of loving, contrasting Falkner's and Elizabeth Raby's childhoods to make her point. After Falkner's mother dies, his early years are marked by unrelieved cruelty and harshness. As a result, he "declared war with my whole soul" (7:159), his

[102]

character marred by a violent nature from which he can never wholly free himself. Elizabeth Raby also suffers after the deaths of her parents. But when Falkner rescues her, she gains both love and extensive education. As a result, she is able to think and take responsibility for herself and for others, and "her love of truth" and "her integrity" give her the independence to defy the social mores of her world when she determines that they are unjust.

Locating *Lodore* and *Falkner* in domestic rather than public spheres of power and politics allowed reviewers to respond to Mary Shelley's works as they had been inclined since the discovery of the female authorship of *Frankenstein*. For the most part, critics treated both novels as love stories: politics, class issues, social values, prisons, education, are largely absent from the reviews though forcefully present in both works. Reviewers understood that *Lodore* and *Falkner* dealt with the responsibility of those on "whom the destiny of others depends" but relegated that moral to the level of parent and child or wife and husband, with no uncomfortable questioning of existent standards. In short, because Mary Shelley transferred the action of her fiction from the public to the personal arena, reviewers confined her subject to the "secrets of the human heart." The contemporary settings of both of her last novels, as well as their use of family politics, have not been generally recognized as consistent with issues of power and politics that bind all her novels together. By and large, critics have ignored the analogous exploration of power as well as its overt exploration, stated in commentaries such as, "[T]he English governors wished to keep [native princes of India] in ignorance and darkness" (*N&SW*, 7:172).

From *Frankenstein* to *Falkner*, Mary Shelley's novels dwell on questions of power, responsibility, and love. The earlier novels largely concentrate on the problems inherent in a world in dramatic transition and are open-ended in their conclusions. Gradually, suggested resolutions, embryonic in *Frankenstein*, augment in her novels until finally, in *Lodore* and *Falkner*, they offer an earthly Promethean vision based on unconditional love and the acceptance of human fallibility. But both *Lodore* and *Falkner* represent fusions of the psychological social novel with the educational novel, resulting not in romances but instead in narratives of destabilization: the heroic protagonists are educated women who strive to create a world of justice and universal love.

It is little wonder that reviewers preferred to emphasize the romance in the story. Like Dickens, whose works were then coming into favor, Mary Shelley presented the injustices of the world. But rather than offer figures who were clearly good or bad, generating transparent reader responses, Mary Shelley continued to delineate complex lives that ultimately challenged and discomforted readers in her commitment to both "educate and elevate." Indeed, Falkner's prison musings on the nature of body and soul return the reader to the paradox of Frankenstein and his Creature:

To the surgeon's eye, a human body sometimes presents itself merely as a mass of bones, muscles, and arteries— though that human body may contain a soul to emulate Shakespear—and thus there are moments when the wretched dissect the forms of life—and contemplating only the outward semblance of events, wonder how so much power of misery, or the reverse, resides in what is after all but sleeping or waking—walking here or walking there—seeing one fellow-creature instead of another. (*N&SW*, 7:280–81)

CHAPTER FOUR

Last Journeys, 1837–1851

ETWEEN 1832 and 1839, while she was completing *Lodore* and *Falkner*, Mary Shelley contributed to five volumes of biographical essays in Rev. Dionysius Lardner's Cabinet of Biography: *Lives of the most Eminent Literary and Scientific Men of Italy, Spain, and Portugal* (1835–37) and *Lives of the most Eminent Literary and Scientific Men of France* (1838–39).[1] These volumes also include essays by James Montgomery (1771–1854) and Sir David Brewster (1781–1868). Mary Shelley's letters identify the authors of many of the essays. For example, referring to volume I of *Lives*, 1835–37, she wrote, "Unfortunately before I was applied to—some of the *best lives* were in other hands— The Omnipresent Mr Montgomery wrote Dante & Ariosto in the present Vol.—the rest are mine."[2] Mary Shelley, then, wrote the essays about Petrarch, Boccaccio, Lorenzo de' Medici, Bojardo, Berni, and Machiavelli. Referring to the first two volumes of the *Lives*, 1835–37, Mary Shelley wrote: "You guessed right as to the sex of Dante's Life; it was written by the Omnipresent Mr Montgomery—as well as Ariosto's . . . the life of Galileo is by Sir David Brewster that of

Tasso by Mʳ Montgomery—the rest are mine & so ends the Italian lives; for which I am sorry. The Spanish & Portugueeze will cost me more trouble, if I can do them at all—There is no Spanish Circulating Library—I cannot while here, read in the Museum."[3]

A number of Mary Shelley's letters trace her efforts to obtain information to compensate for the lack of ready Spanish resources for her essays: "I do not mind trouble—but wish to do my task as well as I can—& how can I without books?—The difficulty seems to be that from slight biographical notices one can yet the book will be more of literature than lives—& I know not how Lardner will like that. The best is that the very thing which occasions the difficulty makes it interesting—namely—the treading in unknown paths & dragging out unknown things—I wish I could go to Spain."[4] To date, the essays about Boscan, Garcilaso de la Vega, Mendoza, Leon, Herrera, Montemayor, Cervantes, Lope de Vega, Espinel, Villegas, Gongora, Quevedo, Calderon, Ribeyra, Vicente, Ferreira, and Camoens have been attributed to Mary Shelley.[5] And a recently published letter indicates that she wrote the life of Ercilla as well.[6]

Mary Shelley acknowledged that she was genuinely interested in the Spanish lives but "not so much" in the French: "[I]t is pleasant writing enough—sparing one's imagination yet occupying one & supplying in some small degree the *needful* which is so very needful." In all, *Lives*, 1838–39, offers biographies of Montaigne, Rabelais, Corneille, Rouchefoucauld, Molière, La Fontaine, Pascal, Sévigné,

Boileau, and Racine in the first volume and of Fénélon, Voltaire, Rousseau, Condorcet, Mirabeau, Roland, and de Staël in the second.[7] Despite her comparative lack of interest in the project, Mary Shelley may have written all the essays in these volumes.

In Mary Shelley's novels *Valperga* and *Perkin Warbeck* she interpolated actual biography with her own fictionalizations to further her political agenda. The *Lives,* like the novels, were carefully researched; and like the novels, they reflect her reformist perspectives. She wrote each life within its historical context, linking the individual with the era. Her letter concerning the writing process and the completed lives themselves also offer a great deal of autobiographical commentary on Mary Shelley's own life and works. For example, in *Lives,* 1838–39, she comments on Madame de Staël's interaction with Byron when he was at Diodati in 1816. Her report of Byron's reactions to de Staël's advice surely derives from the Shelleys' own friendship with Byron that summer. But even more than this kind of factual account, Mary Shelley generalizes her reflection on de Staël's character as she matured to that which "may often be observed with women," giving it important autobiographical overtones: "When young, they are open to such cruel attacks, every step they take in public may bring with it irreparable injury to their private affections, to their delicacy, to their dearest prospects. As years are added they gather courage; they feel the earth grow steadier under their steps; they depend less on others, and their moral worth increases."[8]

Mary Shelley's decreasing interest in the *Lives* may be the result of a far larger, far more significant project that she began during the years in which she wrote the biographies. In 1834 the publisher Edward Moxon opened negotiations with her that would allow her to bring P. B. Shelley's works forward before copyrights expired and his published work passed into the public domain.[9] From that point, though Mary Shelley was not yet free of Sir Timothy's restriction, her correspondence shows that she began the process of borrowing and copying P. B. Shelley's letters for her pro-jected edition. In 1838 her father-in-law, probably hoping that the edition would prevent further increases in funds borrowed for Percy Florence, granted permission for the edition but stipulated that no memoir be included.[10] With Moxon as publisher, between 1839 and 1840 Mary Shelley brought out *The Poetical Works of Percy Bysshe Shelley* in four vol-umes (1839); *Essays, Letters from Abroad, Translations and Fragments by Percy Bysshe Shelley,* in two volumes (1839, dated 1840); and the one-volume edition of *The Poetical Works of Percy Bysshe Shel-ley* (1839, dated 1840).[11]

As she had in the *Posthumous Poems* fifteen years earlier, Mary Shelley, in her prefaces, praises P. B. Shelley's poetic genius and his exemplary moral character. The 1839 pref-ace also expresses more of her own critical judgment of P. B. Shelley's works. She suggests that his poems may be divided into two classes, one purely imaginary, the other comprising those that emanated from the heart (*N&SW,* 2:256). Works in the first category, which she compares to

Plato, pose greater difficulty for those whose minds do not resemble P. B. Shelley's; those in the second category, in which she encouraged him to write but which interested him less, are accessible to a wider audience. Her differentiation drew fire from some critics, who regarded it as an apology rather than a means to introduce the wary to P. B. Shelley. But rather than being an apology, her stratagem emulates both Godwin, who wrote *Caleb Williams* to promulgate his ideology to a wider audience, and also P. B. Shelley, who in writing *The Cenci* believed he wrote for, and would reach, a wider audience. Mary Shelley's preface also demonstrates her continued reformist agenda through its historical appraisal of the political era in which P. B. Shelley lived and his response to it.

Mary Shelley dexterously circumvented Sir Timothy's injunction against biography by appending notes to the works that recalled the circumstances of their composition. Since she had long been in the habit of viewing experience and writing about it historically, her positioning of P. B. Shelley's works within their environment was a particularly congenial format. As a result, the notes provide both a biographical and a historical framework for the poems and remain an invaluable contribution to Shelley studies.

Mary Shelley's work as an editor has been much praised at the same time that certain shortcomings have been realized. Because of the climate of the times, she allowed Moxon to pressure her into omitting atheistic passages of *Queen Mab* to protect his copyright, and she omitted P. B. Shelley's dedication to Harriet Shelley because she believed it was P. B. Shelley's preference.[12] When she convinced Moxon to include the omitted passages in the one-volume edition, he was, as he had feared, tried and found guilty of blasphemous libel, though sentence was not imposed.[13] At times, Mary Shelley worked from imperfect published versions of works rather than from manuscripts; and subsequent critics have noted other flaws in her work, but unquestionably the *Posthumous Poems,* together with the 1839 editions, stand as the turning point in firmly establishing P. B. Shelley as a major author in the English canon.[14]

The notes she began to make towards a full-length biography of P. B. Shelley after his death were incorporated into the notes for the 1839 editions, which kept to the letter of her agreement against biography with Sir Timothy but just as surely violated its spirit. The 1839 notes are in fact biography, informing readers about aspects of P. B. Shelley's life and her own otherwise unavailable. And in keeping her pact with herself to bring P. B. Shelley's works to public recognition, she fulfilled her final collaborative work with Shelley, providing him with professional editorial expertise as years earlier he had provided her.

During the production of the Shelley editions, Mary Shelley suffered the first onset of the intense headaches and pain and paralysis in her arm that grew steadily worse during the last decade of her life, at times incapacitating her for extended periods. Still, in 1844, encouraged by Moxon and by her success with the *History of a Six Weeks' Tour,* and with the impetus to provide funds for an Italian expatriate who would later try to blackmail her,[15] Mary Shelley wrote the two-volume *Rambles in Germany and Italy* (1844). Her last full-length work, *Rambles* is based on letters written during two journeys she made with Percy Florence and several of his friends in 1840 and 1842–43. Unlike most other works in the popular genre of travel memoirs, *Rambles* goes against the grain of the era in its blend of Romantic values, female emancipation, and political advocacy.[16] She amplifies her adventures through a double vision: present experiences heightened by past recollections. Topography becomes the means of self-revelation through which Mary Shelley resists Victorian standards of female decorum as well as her own usual reticence about personal matters.[17]

Her narrative comments on war, national manners, historical perspectives, political observations. The preface to *Rambles* openly associates Mary Shelley's excitement at the prospect of revisiting Italy with the daring adventures of her earlier life, linking these journeys to the life and principles she shared with P. B. Shelley. Just as openly, she describes her habits as an intellectual, independent woman who finds welcome companionship in the written word. She consciously separates *Rambles* from others of the genre and illustrates her self-confidence in her capacity to judge what is new and of special value in *Rambles*. Because Italian cities had been frequently described before, she "was satisfied to select from my letters such portions merely as touched upon subjects that I had not found mentioned elsewhere. It was otherwise as regarded the people, especially in a political point of view; and in treating of them my scope grew more serious" (*N&SW,* 8:65). Her stated objective is to "incite others to regard" the Italians favorably, to arouse interest in their subjugation by the Austro-Hungarian Empire, and to aid them in their fight for independence and liberty. As certainly as P. B. Shelley had instructed readers of *History of a Six Weeks' Tour* in his preface, Mary Shelley instructs her readers.

Of the recent uprisings in Italy, she says that Englishmen in particular "ought to sympathise in their struggles; for the aspiration for free institutions all over the world has its source in England." The French Revolution and the American War of Independence showed the way to "successful resistance to the undue exercise of authority; but the seed was all sown by us" (8:67). Mary Shelley describes the terrible suffering of the Italians under the Austrians but resists a call to arms because armed revolt would disturb the peace of Europe and "Peace is a lovely thing." Echoes of *History of a Six Weeks' Tour* sound in *Rambles* when she talks of the "cottage burnt, the labour of the husbandman destroyed—outrage and death . . . and the fertility and beauty of Italy" that "exaggerate still more the hideousness of the contrast" (8:68). But what is the answer if neither subjugation nor revolution is to be endured? She suggests that "peaceful mediation and a strong universal sense of justice may interpose, instead of the cannon and bayonet" (8:68). Arguing that Italy had been the ground for war from the invasion of Charles VIII until 1815, she links current history and the weakness of papal power to her fictional account of the French and German invasion in *Valperga*. Nine of the ten introductory pages speak of the Italian political situation.

Mary Shelley relied on form and tone to bring her readers, female and male, approving or disapproving of her politics and perspectives, into her circle. *Rambles,* like Wollstonecraft's *Letters from Norway,* is colloquially written in the form of letters to an unidentified friend. They mingle political concern with personal, confessional reflections intertwined with memories of an earlier time when she "dwelt among the early tombs of those" she loved (8:76). Her companions on these rambles, dear to Mary Shelley for their own sakes, also function as keys to the past she shared with P. B. Shelley. Her young companions' interests in sailing, music, and poetry are transfigured into a kind of emotional landscape through which she evokes her own young life, particularly the years in Italy. For Mary Shelley, the journey would "break a chain" that had long held her. Out of England, she would "wander far towards a country which memory painted as a paradise" (8:77). That country was not only Italy; it was the freedom that Italy represented to her. Mary Shelley was again traveling in the country of her imagination.

The first actual journey began in June 1840 and took the travelers from Paris to Metz, down the Moselle to Coblentz, up the Rhine to Mainz, to Frankfurt, Heidelberg,

Baden-Baden, Freiburg, Schaffhausen, Zürich, the
Splügen, and Chiavenna, to settle for two months at Lake
Como. From there they traveled to Milan. At that point
Percy Florence Shelley and his friends returned to Cambridge while Mary Shelley awaited the arrival of funds sufficient for her return journey, which in late September
took her to England via Geneva and Paris. The second
journey, again with Percy Florence and his friends, began
in June 1842 and extended over fourteen months, during
which they traveled to Liège, Cologne, Coblentz, Mainz,
Frankfurt, Kissingen, Berlin, Dresden, Prague, Salzburg,
the Tyrol, Innsbruck, Riva, Verona, Venice, Florence,
Rome, and Sorrento. Their longer stops were at Kissingen, where Mary Shelley tried to restore her health by taking the *kur,* Venice, Florence, Rome, and Sorrento, and
then homeward through Marseilles and Paris.

Rambles presents Mary Shelley as a seasoned traveler who
remarks, sometimes with humor, sometimes with annoy-
ance, on the pleasures and inconveniences of inns, transportation, and food. She is the cultural guide, conversant
with the customs, manners, art collections, music, archi-
tecture, and literary works of the countries visited. But like
Mary Wollstonecraft's, her interests extend well beyond the
ordinary tourist concerns—and well beyond what would be
the normal purview of the female writer. She comments on
women's capacities through illustration: her exhilaration in
wandering the countryside, shooting rapids, canoeing
down a dangerous river, or riding a donkey to explore in

the hills; and her awe and elation in the immense irregularities of the Swiss mountains. She underscores the importance of education by observing the quality of education provided in France, Italy, Germany, and Austria for the poor as well as the privileged, commenting that in Germany, "[t]o our shame . . . the education of the poor is far more attended to" than in England (8:138–39).

Even more unconventional is her attention to economic conditions, discussed in terms of technological and scientific development. She discusses, for example, the effects of the lack of drains in the streets of Paris; cherry trees planted along roadsides to produce kirschwasser; the productivity of farming and its social implications; girls working in silk mills; the new invention of spun glass; her visit to a paper mill; the German development of health spas as a business and German dislike of English doctors who compete there with German doctors; Berlin steel mills; the growth of railroads and their influence on travel. These become a subtheme of her announced major topic: "the people, especially in a political point of view."

On the subjugation of the populace to unfeeling governance, she asks "what act of cruelty and tyranny may not be reacted on the stage of the world, which we boast of as civilized, if one man has uncontrolled power over the lives of the many" (*N&SW*, 8:180). She deplores how the English impressed Hessian troops to fight in the American war for independence as much as she deplores the Napoleonic Bavarian and French oppression of the Tyrol and the tyrannic control of the Austrian empire over Italy. In her call for freedom for individuals and nations and her advocacy of universal education as a means of achieving these ends, she restates in *Rambles* the egalitarian principles expressed in the works of Wollstonecraft and Godwin[18] and her own earlier works. Just as her historical novels *Valperga* and *Perkin Warbeck* voice in fiction her opposition to monarchical government, disapproval of class distinction, abhorrence of slavery and war and their concomitant cruelties, her travel works offer the same arguments in their historical reality.

Because travel for Mary Shelley meant movement and change as opposed to the status quo, she incorporates travel itself as a leitmotif in all her novels. A cosmopolitan internationalist, she viewed other cultures as opportunities to explore basic concepts of existence and alternate perspectives. If variations already exist, other variations are possible, opening the way to social and political reform. She is ever Lionel Verney of *The Last Man,* for whom "[p]oetry and its creations, philosophy and its researches and classifications, alike awoke the sleeping ideas in my mind, and gave me new ones" (*N&SW,* 4:27). *Rambles* represents what is "generally called the world of reality" as well as the "awakening to a new country to find that there was a deeper meaning in all I saw, besides that which my eyes conveyed to me" (*The Last Man, N&SW,* 4:27).

As she was completing *Rambles,* an event occurred that changed Mary Shelley's life. On 24 April 1844 Sir Timothy Shelley died. The baronetcy passed to Percy Florence Shelley, and he and Mary Shelley together inherited the entailed estate. Though they found its net worth considerably depleted, and they had to repay to Sir Timothy Shelley's other heirs the allowance received for Percy Florence Shelley since 1823, for the first time since P. B. Shelley's death Mary Shelley was financially secure. In 1848 Sir Percy and Jane Gibson St. John were married, bringing to Mary Shelley a loving and beloved daughter-in-law whose background was in its way as unconventional as Mary Shelley's own. Jane Gibson was one of nine illegitimate children of Ann Shevill (?1790–c. 1866 at least) and Thomas Gibson (1759–1832), a wealthy banker; and she was the widow of Charles Robert St. John (1807–44), son of George Richard St. John, third viscount Bolingbroke and fourth viscount St. John (1761–1824), who fathered fifteen children, only four of whom (including Charles Robert) were legitimate.[19]

Mary Shelley's last years reflect her energy of mind and spirit, despite her cycles of severely impaired health. She, Sir Percy, and Jane, Lady Shelley, lived and traveled together. Nor was her professional writing confined only to *Rambles.* During the 1840s she continued to emend the Shelley editions. As late as February 1850 she translated several chapters from an Italian novel by Laura Galloni (nee Mason) and offered to do more.[20] And she returned to the major project that she had begun years earlier: her biography of P. B. Shelley.

Despite Sir Timothy's restrictions, Mary Shelley's letters over the years reflect her continued determination to write the biography. By 1829, however, her understanding of English society had convinced her that the public was not yet ready to accept the true story of P. B. Shelley's life, and she was unwilling to offer less.[21] Out of concern for her son and Ianthe Esdaile, among others, she determined that the biography would not be published in either her own or her son's lifetime.[22] The adverse reaction of reviewers and friends to Godwin's *Memoirs* of Mary Wollstonecraft almost certainly influenced Mary Shelley's decision. But Godwin's candor also apparently set a standard that Mary Shelley wished to realize in her biography of P. B. Shelley.

Serious illness, first her daughter-in-law's and then her own, prevented Mary Shelley from fulfilling her objective. On 1 February 1851, already in a coma for a week, Mary Shelley succumbed to the brain tumor that she had struggled with for about a decade. In deference to her wish to be buried with her parents, Sir Percy had Godwin's and Wollstonecraft's remains disinterred from St. Pancras Churchyard. On 8 February, Mary Shelley's remains and those of her parents were entombed in St. Peter's Churchyard, Bournemouth, near Boscombe Manor, the younger Shelleys' estate.

Her son and daughter-in-law were to play a significant role in "Victorianizing" Mary Shelley through controlling, to the extent they could, biographies written about both P. B. Shelley and Mary Shelley and suppressing and even destroying letters.[23] Just as P. B. Shelley in that era was portrayed as "an ineffectual angel" rather than the radical he was,[24] Mary Shelley's reconstructed reputation further dislocated her from her reformist politics and unconventional life. Ironically, her own family extended the work of depoliticization and domestication that the critics of her novels had begun years earlier with the discovery that a woman, not a man, had written *Frankenstein*. So efficient was the filter of the era that even today Mary Shelley is often depicted as a victim of conventional expectations for women, the inherent dissonance of her works glossed over as ambiguous subservience or psychological affliction.[25]

No doubt one major cause of such readings has been the relative unavailability of Mary Shelley's novels, with the exceptions of *Frankenstein* and *The Last Man*. The Pickering edition for the first time offers modern readers the opportunity to explore the novels, travel works, essays, introductions, prefaces, and miscellaneous pieces as a whole, supplemented by Charles Robinson's edition of her collected tales and short stories. Other editions of various of her works are also being published. Contextualized in terms of *The Letters of Mary Wollstonecraft Shelley* and *The Journals of Mary Shelley, 1814–1844*, these editions provide the basis for a new reading of Mary Shelley and for validating Mary Shelley as a Romantic who outlived her peers but not her Romantic principles or her claim to be recognized among "the Elect" of nineteenth-century literature and political reform.

Chronology

1756

3 March   Birth of William Godwin

1759

27 April   Birth of Mary Wollstonecraft

1768   Birth of Mary Jane Vial (Clairmont)

1792

4 August   Birth of Percy Bysshe Shelley

1794

14 May   Birth of Fanny Imlay Godwin

1795

4 June   Birth of Charles Gaulis Clairmont

1797

29 March   William Godwin and Mary Wollstonecraft marry at Old St. Pancras Church, London

6 April   Godwins take apartment at 29 The Polygon; Godwin takes rooms at 17 Evesham Building, Chalton Street

30 August   Birth of Mary Wollstonecraft Godwin

| 10 September | Death of Mary Wollstonecraft |
| 15 September | Burial of Mary Wollstonecraft at churchyard of Old St. Pancras Church |

1798

| 27 April | Birth of Clara Mary Jane (Claire) Clairmont |

1801

| 5 May | Godwin meets Mary Jane Clairmont |
| 21 December | Godwin marries Mary Jane Clairmont, who brings with her a son, Charles, and a daughter, Clara Mary Jane (later Claire) |

1803

| 28 March | Birth of William Godwin Jr. |

1807

| 13 November | Godwins move to 41 Skinner Street |

1808

| January | *Mounseer Nongtongpaw* published, incorporating Mary Godwin's draft |

1811

| 17 May–
19 December | Mary Godwin at Ramsgate for sea-bathing to cure infected arm |

1812

| 7 June | Mary Godwin sent by Godwin to live in Dundee with the family of a Scottish friend, William Baxter |

10 November	Mary Godwin returns with Christy Baxter to Godwin's Skinner Street home for a visit
11 November	Mary Godwin meets P. B. Shelley and his wife Harriet Westbrook Shelley at Skinner Street

1813

3 June	Mary Godwin and Christy Baxter return to Dundee
23 June	Eliza Ianthe Shelley born to Harriet and P. B. Shelley

1814

30 March	Mary Godwin returns to Skinner Street from Scotland
13 May	Mary Godwin and P. B. Shelley meet again
28 July	Mary Godwin and P. B. Shelley, accompanied by her stepsister Claire Clairmont, elope to the Continent
July–August	Travel through France, Switzerland, Germany, and Holland; source of *History of a Six Weeks' Tour*
13 September	Mary Godwin, P. B. Shelley, and Claire Clairmont return to London
October–November	P. B. Shelley in danger of arrest for debt
30 November	Birth of Charles Shelley, second child of P. B. Shelley and Harriet Shelley

1815

5 January	Death of Sir Bysshe Shelley, P. B. Shelley's grandfather
22 February	Birth of Mary Godwin and P. B. Shelley's first daughter
6 March	Death of daughter
April	Chancery suit to establish Sir Timothy Shelley's rights over disposal of Sir Bysshe's estate
13 May	Provisional settlement with P. B. Shelley's father; P. B. Shelley to receive £1,000 per year, P. B. Shelley arranges for estranged wife to receive £200 per year
June	Mary Godwin and P. B. Shelley tour southern coast of England and Devon
August	Mary Godwin and P. B. Shelley reside at Bishopsgate
Winter	At Bishopsgate; P. B. Shelley writes *Alastor*

1816

24 January	Birth of William Shelley
February	*Alastor* published
April	Second Chancery suit regarding P. B. Shelley's grandfather's estate; Claire Clairmont and Byron become lovers

3 May	Mary Godwin, P. B. Shelley, William Shelley, and Claire Clairmont depart for Switzerland to meet Byron
17 May	Mary Godwin, P. B. Shelley, and party in Switzerland; live near Byron
c. 16 June	Mary Godwin begins *Frankenstein*; P. B. Shelley and Byron travel around Lake Geneva
21 July	Mary Godwin, P. B. Shelley, and Claire Clairmont to Chamonix
29 August	Mary Godwin, P. B. Shelley, William Shelley, and Claire Clairmont leave for England
8 September	Mary Godwin, P. B. Shelley, William Shelley, and Claire Clairmont return to England and lodge in Bath
9 October	Fanny Godwin commits suicide
c. 10 December	Harriet Shelley commits suicide
15 December	News of Harriet Shelley's suicide reaches P. B. Shelley
30 December	Mary Godwin and P. B. Shelley marry at St. Mildred's, Bread Street, London

1817

12 January	Birth of Claire Clairmont and Byron's daughter, Allegra
January	Shelleys move to London

January–July 1818	Chancery suit over guardianship of P. B. Shelley and Harriet Shelley's children, Ianthe and Charles
March	Shelleys reside at Albion House, Marlow
27 March	P. B. Shelley denied custody of Ianthe and Charles in Chancery Court proceedings
April–December	Mary Shelley finishes *Frankenstein;* begins *History of a Six Weeks' Tour*
May	P. B. Shelley writes *Laon and Cythna*
2 September	Birth of daughter Clara Everina Shelley
December–January	*History of a Six Weeks' Tour* and *The Revolt of Islam* published

1818

1 January	*Frankenstein* published
January–February	Albion House sold; Shelleys and Claire Clairmont move to London
11 March	Shelleys, Claire Clairmont, and Allegra depart for Italy
4 April	Arrive in Milan

May	Shelleys and Claire Clairmont to Pisa and Leghorn; meet Gisbornes
11 June	Move to Casa Bertini, Bagni di Lucca
17 August	P. B. Shelley and Claire Clairmont go to Venice and Este
5 September	Mary Shelley and children join them at Este; P. B. Shelley begins *Prometheus Unbound*
24 September	Clara Shelley dies in Venice
29 October	Allegra sent to Byron in Venice
5 November	The Shelleys and Claire Clairmont travel to Rome and remain until late November; leave for Naples
1819	
March	Reside in Rome
May	P. B. Shelley begins *The Cenci*; Mary Shelley translates manuscript, source of P. B. Shelley's *Cenci*
7 June	William Shelley dies in Rome
June	Move to Leghorn, then Villa Valsovano, near Montenero
August	Mary Shelley begins *Matilda*
October	Reside at 4395 Via Valfonda, Florence
12 November	Birth of Percy Florence Shelley

1820

January	Move to Casa Frasi, Pisa
March–April	Mary Shelley begins *Castruccio, Prince of Lucca* (*Valperga*); *The Cenci* published
April–	Mary Shelley writes mythological drama *Proserpine*
c. May	Mary Shelley writes mythological drama *Midas*
June 15	Move to Leghorn
August	Move to Casa Prinni, Bagni San Giuliano; *Prometheus Unbound* published
October	Reside at Palazzo Galetti, Pisa
November	Meet Emilia Viviani

1821

January	Shelleys meet Edward and Jane Williams
February–March	Shelleys move to Casa Aulla, Pisa; P. B. Shelley write *Epipsychidion*
May	Return to Bagni San Giuliano; *Epipsychidion* published
October	Return to Pisa
November	Byron arrives in Pisa

1822

January	Edward John Trelawny arrives in Pisa
31 January	Godwin accepts Mary Shelley's offer to publish *Castruccio* for his benefit
19 April	Allegra Byron dies at Bagnacavallo
30 April	Move, with Williamses, to Casa Magni, San Terenzo
16 June	Mary Shelley has miscarriage
1 July	P. B. Shelley and Edward Williams sail to Leghorn to welcome Leigh Hunt and family to Italy
8 July	P. B. Shelley and Williams drown in Gulf of Spezia returning from Leghorn
20 July	Mary Shelley and Jane Williams remove to Pisa
16 August	P. B. Shelley's body cremated at Viareggio
11 September	Mary Shelley to Genoa; rents Casa Negroto
17 September	Jane Williams leaves for London
20 September	Claire Clairmont departs for Vienna
3 October	Byron arrives in Genoa; settles in Casa Saluzzo
4 October	Hunt and family join Mary Shelley at Casa Negroto

1823

21 January	P. B. Shelley's ashes interred in the Protestant Cemetery, Rome
6 February	Sir Timothy Shelley writes to Byron to offer to assume the guardianship of Percy Florence Shelley if Mary Shelley relinquishes custody; refuses Mary Shelley support
19 February	*Valperga* published
25 February	Mary Shelley refuses Sir Timothy Shelley's offer regarding Percy Florence Shelley's custody
? July	Mary Shelley writes poem "The Choice"
24 July	Byron and Trelawny sail for Greece
25 July	Mary Shelley and Percy Florence Shelley leave Genoa for England
12-20 August	Mary Shelley in Paris
25 August	Mary Shelley returns to London
29 August	Mary Shelley sees adaptation of *Frankenstein*, which Godwin arranged to be republished
3 September	Whitton advances Mary Shelley £100
8 September	Moves to 14 Speldhurst Street, Brunswick Square

27 November	Mary Shelley receives repayable allowance for support of Percy Florence of £100 per year from Sir Timothy Shelley
Winter	Begins *The Last Man*

1824

19 April	Death of Byron in Greece
June	Mary Shelley's edition of *Posthumous Poems of Percy Bysshe Shelley* published; Sir Timothy objects strongly; by August 22, after the sale of more than three hundred copies, Mary Shelley agrees to suppress the remaining copies in order to retain allowance for Percy Florence
21 June	Resides at 5 Bartholomew Place, Kentish Town, near Jane Williams
9 July	Views Byron's body before burial
August	£200 per year allowance from Sir Timothy Shelley begins

1826

23 January	*The Last Man* published
August	Spends month in Brighton with Jane Williams
14 September	Death of Charles Shelley; Percy Florence becomes heir to baronetcy

1827	
May	Allowance increased to £250 per year
2 June	Mary Shelley renews acquaintance with Thomas Moore
July	Discovery of Jane Williams's betrayal
July–October	Mary Shelley at Sompting, Arundel, with Isabella Robinson and Mary Diana Dods ("Mr. and Mrs. Walter Sholto Douglas")
September	Percy Florence Shelley attends day school in Arundel
End of October	Moves to 51 George Street, Portman Square
1828	
11 February	Confrontation with Jane Williams
25 March	Percy Florence Shelley attends Mr. Slater's school, Kensington
11 April	Mary Shelley to Paris to visit "Douglases"; ill with smallpox; meets Prosper Mérimée, General Lafayette, and others in Garnett circle
26 May	Leaves Paris
June–August	Recuperation at Dover and Hastings

7 August	Resides at Park Cottage, Paddington, with Robinsons
16 October	Claire Clairmont returns to London
15 November	Reunion with Trelawny
24 December	Moves to 4 Oxford Terrace, London
1829 May–	
January 1830	Secretly assists Cyrus Redding in publication of the Galignanis' edition of P. B. Shelley's poems in Paris
May	Moves to 33 Somerset Street, Portman Square
1 June	Allowance from Sir Timothy Shelley increased to £300 per year for Percy Florence Shelley
18 September	Claire Clairmont leaves for Dresden
1830 February	William Godwin Jr. and Emily Eldred marry
13 May	*The Fortunes of Perkin Warbeck* published
July	Resides at Southend
August– October	At Park Cottage

1831

November | Revised edition of *Frankenstein* published

1832 | *Proserpine* published (*Midas,* her other drama, first published in 1922)

Mid-June–
mid-September | Resides at Sandgate

1 August | Trelawny visits Mary Shelley; Maria Julia Trelawny stays until mid-September

8 September | Death of William Godwin Jr.

29 September | Percy Florence Shelley enters Harrow

1833

May | Moves to Harrow; Percy Florence Shelley becomes a day student

4 May | Godwin awarded sinecure as Yeoman Usher of the Exchequer; moves to 15 New Palace Yard

1835

February | First volume of *Lives of the Most Eminent Literary and Scientific Men of Italy, Spain and Portugal* published

7 April | *Lodore* published

October | Second volume of *Lives of the Most Eminent Literary and Scientific Men of Italy, Spain and Portugal* published

1836

7 April	Death of William Godwin
April	Mary Shelley moves to 14 North Bank, Regents Park, London

1837

February	*Falkner* published
March Street	Mary Shelley moves to 24 South Audley
October	Percy Florence Shelley enters Trinity College, Cambridge
November	Mary Shelley moves to 41d Park Street, Grosvenor Square

1838

c. August	Sir Timothy lifts the ban he imposed on Mary Shelley's publication of P. B. Shelley's works
August	First volume of *Lives of the Most Eminent Literary and Scientific Men of France* published

1839

January	Beginning of periods of illness that last until Mary Shelley's death in 1851
January–May	Publication of *Poetical Works of Percy Bysshe Shelley*, 4 volumes

March	Resides at Layton House, Putney
August	Second volume of *Lives of the Most Eminent Literary and Scientific Men of France* published
November	Publication of Mary Shelley's edition of *Poetical Works of Percy Bysshe Shelley*, 1 volume
December	Publication of P. B. Shelley's *Essays, Letters from Abroad, Translations and Fragments*

1840
June—
early January — Tour of the Continent with Percy Florence Shelley, his friends: Cadenabbia, Milan, and Paris

1841
January — Resides at 84 Park Street, London; Percy Florence Shelley graduates from Trinity College; gift from Sir Timothy Shelley to Percy Florence of £400 per year

17 June — Death of Mary Jane Clairmont

1842
June—
30 August 1843 — Tour of the Continent with Percy Florence Shelley, Alexander Knox, and Henry Hugh Pearson: Kissingen, Berlin, Dresden, Venice, Florence, Rome, and Paris

1843

September — Moves to White Cottage, Putney

1844

24 April — Death of Sir Timothy Shelley; Mary Shelley and Percy Florence Shelley inherit estate; Percy Florence inherits title

July — *Rambles in Germany and Italy* published

1845

September — Attempted blackmail of Mary Shelley by Ferdinand Gatteschi

October — Attempted blackmail of Mary Shelley by George "Byron"

1846

c. March — Moves to 24 Chester Square

1848

22 June — Sir Percy Florence Shelley marries Jane St. John

August — Shelleys move to Field Place

1849

September–
May 1850 — To Continent with Percy Florence Shelley and Jane Shelley: Paris, Nice, Cadinabbia

1851

1 February — Death of Mary Shelley, Chester Square; buried, St. Peter's, Bournemouth, near

(1 February)   Percy Florence Shelley and Jane Shelley's new home at Boscombe. To comply with Mary Shelley's wish that she be buried beside her parents, the remains of William Godwin and Mary Wollstonecraft are removed to St. Peter's; Percy Florence Shelley died on 5 December 1889, Jane Shelley, on 24 June 1899; both are interred in the same grave as Mary Shelley and her parents

Notes

CHAPTER ONE · Early Journeys, 1797–1818

1. Manuscript journal of William Godwin, 1788–1836, Abinger Collection, Bodleian Library (hereafter cited as Godwin, Journal).

2. Mary Wollstonecraft, *The Works of Mary Wollstonecraft,* ed. Marilyn Butler and Janet Todd, 7 vols. (London: Pickering & Chatto, 1989), vols. 5 and 6.

3. Kenneth Neill Cameron, Donald H. Reiman, and Doucet Devin Fischer, eds., *Shelley and His Circle, 1773–1822,* 8 vols. to date (Cambridge: Harvard University Press, 1961–), 1:445–47 (hereafter cited as *S&C*); William Godwin, *The Political and Philosophical Writings of William Godwin,* ed. Martin Fitzpatrick with an introduction by Mark Philp, 7 vols. (London: Pickering & Chatto, 1993), 1:13.

4. E.g., Gary Kelly, *The Mind and Career of Mary Wollstonecraft* (New York: St. Martin's Press, 1992); and Paula R. Backscheider and Timothy Dystal, eds., *The Intersections of the Public and Private Spheres in Early Modern England* (London: Frank Cass, 1996).

5. See, e.g., Patricia Meyer Spacks, *The Female Imagination* (New York: Avon Books, 1975); Ellen Moers, *Literary*

Women: The Great Writers (New York: Anchor Books, 1977); San-
dra M. Gilbert and Susan Gubar, *The Madwoman in the Attic* (New
Haven: Yale Univ. Press, 1979); and Audrey A. Fisch, Anne K.
Mellor, and Esther H. Schor, eds., *The Other Mary Shelley: Beyond
Frankenstein* (New York: Oxford Univ. Press, 1993). For a dis-
cussion of the modern reception of Mary Shelley's works, see
Betty T. Bennett, "Feminism and Editing Mary Wollstonecraft
Shelley: The Editor and?/or? the Text," in *Palimpsest: Editorial
Theory in the Humanities,* ed. George Bornstein and Ralph G. Wil-
liams (Ann Arbor: Univ. of Michigan Press, 1993), 67–96.

6. William St Clair, *The Godwins and the Shelleys: The Biography of a
Family* (London: Faber & Faber, 1989), 73.

7. Sources drawn on for this discussion include: Marilyn But-
ler, *Romantics, Rebels, and Reactionaries* (New York: Oxford Univ.
Press, 1982); Elie Halévy, *England in 1815* (New York: Barnes &
Noble, 1961); E. J. Hobsbawm, *The Age of Revolution: 1789–1848*
(New York: Mentor, 1962); Harold Perkin, *The Origins of Modern
English Society: 1780–1880* (London: Routledge & Kegan Paul,
1969); E. P. Thompson, *The Making of the English Working Class* (New
York: Vintage Books, 1963); and Fernand Braudel, *The Structures
of Everyday Life: Civilization and Capitalism, Fifteenth to Eighteenth Century,*
trans. Sian Reynolds (New York: Harper & Row, 1981).

8. See, e.g., Wollstonecraft, *Works,* 1:16; and William Godwin,
Collected Novels and Memoirs of William Godwin, ed. Mark Philp, 8 vols.
(London: Pickering & Chatto, 1992), 1:18–19.

9. For discussions of P. B. Shelley's philosophy of love, see
S&C, 2:612–14; Frederick Beatty, *Light from Heaven* (DeKalb:
Northern Illinois Univ. Press, 1971), 169–74ff.; and Nathaniel

Browne, *Sexuality and Feminism in Shelley* (Cambridge: Harvard Univ. Press, 1979).

10. For the most up-to-date listing of Mary Shelley's poems and their publications, see Mary Shelley, *The Novels and Selected Works of Mary Shelley*, gen. ed. Nora Crook with Pamela Clemit, consulting ed. Betty T. Bennett, 8 vols. (London: William Pickering, 1996), 1:lxxx–lxxxvii (hereafter cited as *N&SW*); and Betty T. Bennett, "Newly Uncovered Letters and Poems by Mary Wollstonecraft Shelley," *Keats-Shelley Journal* 46 (1997): 72–74.

11. Mary Shelley, *The Letters of Mary Wollstonecraft Shelley*, ed. Betty T. Bennett, 3 vols. (Baltimore: Johns Hopkins Univ. Press, 1980–88), 2:246 (hereafter cited as *MWSL*).

12. Godwin, Journal, records that on the night before her death, Mary Wollstonecraft and he spoke of "Mary and Fanny."

13. See esp. *The Enquirer,* in Godwin, *Political and Philosophical Writings,* vol. 5, ed. Pamela Clemit.

14. The private pupil was Willis Webb (see C. Kegan Paul, *William Godwin: His Friends and Contemporaries,* 2 vols. [London: Henry S. King & Co., 1876], 1:32–35). On Cooper, see Paul, *Godwin,* 1:35–46; and Don Locke, *A Fantasy of Reason* (London: Routledge & Kegan Paul, 1980), 33–39.

15. Published in London by J. Johnson in 1787, 1789, and 1792, respectively. Reprinted in Wollstonecraft, *Works,* vols. 4 and 5.

16. See, e.g., Ford K. Brown, *The Life of William Godwin* (London: J. M. Dent & Sons, 1926), 177 and other letters cited; Paul,

Godwin, 2:74 and other letters cited; as well as unpublished Godwin letters, in Abinger Collection.

17. Godwin, *Political and Philosophical Writings,* 1:38.

18. St Clair, *The Godwins,* 199—204.

19. St Clair, *The Godwins,* 241.

20. *MWSL,* 2:215.

21. Two inventories of Godwin's library are extant: his "Catalogue of Godwin's Library in His own Handwriting—in 1817," in the Keats-Shelley Memorial House, Rome, and *Catalogue of the Curious Library of that Very Eminent and Distinguished Author, William Godwin, Esq.* (London, 1836), sold at auction by Mr. Sotheby and Son on 17—18 June 1836. On the portrait of Mary Wollstonecraft, see St Clair, *The Godwins,* 180.

22. Claire Clairmont, Charles Clairmont, and Fanny Imlay Godwin, *The Clairmont Correspondence: Letters of Claire Clairmont, Charles Clairmont, and Fanny Imlay Godwin,* ed. Marion Kingston Stocking, 2 vols. (Baltimore: Johns Hopkins Univ. Press, 1995), 1:295. For a listing of some of Claire Clairmont's own efforts at writing, see Claire Clairmont, *The Journals of Claire Clairmont,* ed. Marion Kingston Stocking with David Mackenzie Stocking (Cambridge: Harvard Univ. Press, 1968), 532, "Writings."

23. Nicholson (1753—1815) and Godwin met in 1786 and remained particular friends until the former's death. An experimental scientist, inventor, and author of respected scientific books, Nicholson is credited with pioneering work in the area of electricity *(Dictionary of National Biography).* Mary Wollstonecraft and Thomas Holcroft had translated Johann Kaspar Lavater's

Essays in Physiognomy, a theory that linked human expression to human emotions. At this time Godwin was particularly interested in phrenology, which used the shape of the skull as a method to understand human psychology (St Clair, *The Godwins,* 262).

24. William Nicholson to William Godwin, 18 September 1797, in Paul, *Godwin,* 1:289–90.

25. "On Phrenology" (1831), in *Thoughts on Man,* vol. 6 of Godwin, *Political and Philosophical Writings,* 231–40; see Locke, *Fantasy of Reason,* 219, 320–23.

26. All references to Mary Shelley's works are to *N&SW* (see above, n. 10).

27. St Clair, *The Godwins,* 284–93.

28. St Clair, *The Godwins,* 285. He had earlier published children's books under the name William Scolfield.

29. Mary Wollstonecraft, *Posthumous Works of the Author of a Vindication of the Rights of Woman,* 4 vols. (London: J. Johnson & G. G. and J. Robinson, 1798); idem, *Memoirs of the Author of a Vindication of the Rights of Woman* (London: J. Johnson & G. G. and J. Robinson, 1798), 2nd edition revised 1798.

30. Wollstonecraft, *Works,* 1:16; Godwin, *Collected Novels,* 1:16–17; St Clair, *The Godwins,* 184–88.

31. *MWSL,* 2:3–4; see also *MWSL,* 1:4, 376. The words "of my life" were deleted by Mary Shelley.

32. It appears that Godwin informed Fanny Imlay Godwin of her true parentage when she was eleven: "Explanation w. Fanny" (Godwin, Journal, 8 February 1806). She may have spoken of

it to her half-sister while both were still young. The extent of Godwin's explanation of her parentage is unclear. Nor is it clear when Mary Shelley found out that her own parents married only five months before her own birth. Copies of the *Memoirs* as well as *Posthumous Works* and *Letters from Norway* were accessible in Godwin's own study, which he inventoried in 1817 ("Catalogue of Godwin's Library," 1817; see above, n. 21). Mary Shelley, *The Journals of Mary Shelley, 1814–1844,* ed. Paula R. Feldman and Diana Scott-Kilvert, 2 vols. (Oxford: Clarendon Press, 1987; Baltimore: Johns Hopkins Univ. Press, 1995) (hereinafter cited as *MWSJ*), lists a number of her mother's works that she read in the years following the Shelleys' elopement, but the *Memoirs* are not listed in the extant *MWSJ*.

33. Godwin to E. Fordham, 13 November 1811, Abinger Collection, quoted in part in Paul, *Godwin,* 2:213–14.

34. *Vindication,* in Wollstonecraft, *Works,* 5:90.

35. See, e.g., *MWSJ,* 2:543.

36. *MWSJ,* 2:479.

37. Paul, *Godwin,* 2:214. See also *S&C,* 3:100–101, for Godwin's high estimation of Mary Shelley's capabilities.

38. See, e.g., Godwin's introduction to *The History of England* (London: M. J. Godwin & Co., 1806), vi, in which he speaks of his theories and of reading the book to his children.

39. For the most complete bibliography of Godwin's children's works, see St Clair, *The Godwins.*

40. Netting is a process of knotting tiny ropes to make a

meshed fabric, "formerly used esp. of making small, fancy-work articles, such as purses" (*Oxford English Dictionary*, 2nd ed.).

41. Emily W. Sunstein, *Mary Shelley: Romance and Reality* (Boston: Little, Brown, 1989; reprint, Baltimore: Johns Hopkins Univ. Press, 1991), 48, 103.

42. *MWSL*, 3:83–84.

43. Godwin, Journal, entry for 17 May 1811 reads, "MJ, M & W for Margate" [*sic*]; and for 19 December 1811, "MWG in Skinner Street."

44. See Muriel Spark, *Child of Light: A Reassessment of Mary Shelley* (Hadleigh, Essex: Tower Bridge Publications, 1951), revised as *Mary Shelley* (New York: E. P. Dutton, 1987); and Sunstein, *Mary Shelley*, 54–55.

45. For example, James Marshall, Godwin's boyhood friend, referred to Mary Jane Godwin as a "clever, bustling, second-rate woman, glib of tongue and pen, with a temper undisciplined and uncontrolled; not bad-hearted, but with a complete absence of all the finer sensibilities" (St Clair, *The Godwins*, 244–45).

46. St Clair, *The Godwins*, 245.

47. Godwin, Journal.

48. Lady Mount Cashell to William Godwin, 6 August 1801, Abinger Collection; Sunstein, *Mary Shelley*, 24, 26.

49. Clairmont attended the Charterhouse School from c. 1804 to 1811 (see *Clairmont Correspondence*, cited in n. 22, above, 1:1); and William Godwin Jr. attended a Roman Catholic

school, Charterhouse School, Dr. Burney's school at Green-
wich, and Mr. Jay's "commercial establishment" (see Paul, *Godwin*, 2:257–58; and St Clair, *The Godwins*, 297–98).

50. The boarding house was at Walham Green (see Clairmont,
Journals, 20).

51. Aaron Burr, *The Private Journal*, ed. Matthew L. Davis, 2 vols.
(New York: Harper & Brothers, 1838), 2:307.

52. See *MWSL*, 1:5 n. 2.

53. Sunstein, *Mary Shelley*, 56–61.

54. P. B. Shelley, dedication to *Laon and Cythna* (1817), later *The
Revolt of Islam* (1818), stanza 1, line 9.

55. *MWSJ*, 2:443.

56. *The Letters of Percy Bysshe Shelley*, ed. Frederick L. Jones, 2 vols.
(Oxford: Clarendon Press, 1964), 1:402 (hereafter cited as
PBSL).

57. St Clair, *The Godwins*, 362.

58. Clairmont, *Journals*, 20–21.

59. *MWSJ*, 1:15.

60. Mary Shelley continued her journals until 1844.

61. *MWSJ*, 1:8.

62. Newman Ivey White, *Shelley*, 2 vols., rev. ed. (London:
Secker & Warburg, 1947), 1:364–71.

63. *MWSL*, 3:92, 84.

64. *S&C*, 4:605–9; White, *Shelley*, 1:393–99.

65. *S&C*, 4:769–802; Kenneth Neill Cameron, *Shelley: The Golden Years* (Cambridge: Harvard Univ. Press, 1974), 42–43, 147n, 578.

66. See *MWSL*, 1:24–25; *PBSL*, 1:524–25, 539–40; and *S&C*, 5:391–92.

67. Roger Ingpen, *Shelley in England: New Facts and Letters from the Shelley-Whitton Papers*, 2 vols. (Boston: Houghton Mifflin, 1917), 2:422–24.

68. White, *Shelley*, 1:495.

69. *MWSL*, 1:4–5.

70. *MWSL*, 1:29.

71. See, e.g., Godwin to P. B. Shelley, 10 December 1812, MS. Shelley, adds. c. 524, Bodleian Library.

72. E.g., see the discussion of *The Cenci* and *Proserpine* below.

73. Introduction to *Frankenstein* (1831), *N&SW*, 1:176.

74. Charles E. Robinson, "Percy Bysshe Shelley, Charles Ollier, and William Blackwood," in *Shelley Revalued*, ed. Kelvin Everest (Totowa, N.J.: Barnes & Noble, 1983), 192.

75. See the discussion of *The Last Man* in chapter 3, below, for references to Mary Shelley's own commentary on the uses of autobiography in literary works.

76. Thomas Moore was among those who recognized the authorship (see *PBSL*, 1:582).

77. *MWSJ*, 1:22.

78. E.g., *MWSJ*, 1:13.

79. *MWSJ*, 13.

80. See, e.g., Wollstonecraft, *Works*, 6:248, on how Mary Wollstonecraft asked "men's questions"; Leigh Hunt in *The Examiner*, 5 October 1817, 626 (see also *MWSL*, 1:54); and the review of *Rambles* in *New Monthly Magazine* 72 (1844): 284—86.

81. *MWSL*, 1:20.

82. Mary Shelley received the completed volumes on 31 December 1817 (*MWSJ*). For a transcription and an in-depth discussion of the *Frankenstein* manuscripts, see Mary Shelley, *The Frankenstein Notebooks,* ed. Charles E. Robinson, 2 vols., The Manuscripts of the Younger Romantics, ed. Donald H. Reiman, 9 (New York: Garland, 1996).

83. Though the second edition was prepared by Godwin, apparently without Mary Shelley's direct input, she later indicated her approval of Godwin's suggested changes by incorporating them into her 1831 revisions (see *N&SW*, vol. 1, introductory note).

84. *Fantasmagoriana, ou recueil d'histoires apparitions de spectres, revenans, fantômes, etc.; Traduit de l'allemand, par un amateur,* 2 vols. (Paris: Lenormant et Schoell, 1812), Jean Baptiste Benoît Eyriès's translation of the German *Der Gespensterbuch,* 5 vols. Translated into English as *Tales of the Dead* (London: White, Cochrane, & Co., 1813), it is available as *Tales of the Dead: The Ghost Stories of the Villa Diodati,* ed. Terry Hale (Chislehurst: The Gothic Society at the Gargoyle's Head Press, 1992).

85. Godwin's 1799 novel *St. Leon* was set in Switzerland and south Germany and treated the subject of the secret of life. It

has a character named Marguerite, the wife of the central figure. St. Leon's fall is the result of his self-centered quest for
the key to all knowledge, in the course of which he sacrifices the
lives of his wife and child (Godwin, *Collected Novels*, 1:31).

86. See St Clair, *The Godwins*, for an in-depth discussion of
Godwin and science.

87. See, e.g., Mary Shelley's manuscript recounting P. B.
Shelley's boyhood experiments with science, including "a galvanic battery" and the "charnel house" (MS. Shelley, adds. c.
5, fol. 116, Bodleian Library); and *PBSL*, 1:227, 303.

88. *MWSJ*, 1:142–44; see also Laura E. Crouch, "Davy's *A Discourse, Introductory to A Course of Lectures on Chemistry*: A Possible Scientific Source for Frankenstein," *Keats–Shelley Journal* 27 (1978):
35–44.

89. See *PBSL*, 2:472, for P. B. Shelley's reading of Davy and
Darwin.

90. Brown, *William Godwin*, 128; David Knight, *Humphry Davy*
(London: Blackwell, 1992), 121–22.

91. St Clair, *The Godwins*, 61.

92. For discussions of the close link between science and politics in this era, see Halévy, *England in 1815*, 552–71; and Colin
Russell, *Science and Social Change, 1700–1900* (London: Macmil-
lan, 1983).

93. William Gilbert, *De Magnete [On the Magnet . . . a New Physiology,
Demonstrated by Many Arguments and Experiments]*, 1600.

94. Gilbert, *De Magnete*, ch. 12.

95. As P. B. Shelley actually had as a boy (see above, n. 87).

96. *MWSL*, 1:401.

CHAPTER TWO · Italy, 1818—1823

1. See *MWSL*, 1:149.

2. See *MWSL*, 1:6—7.

3. See *MWSL*, 1:223, for Mary Shelley's parody of a nursery rhyme applied to "la Italiana."

4. The story was published in the *London Magazine* 9 (April 1824): 357—63; it is reprinted in *Mary Shelley: Collected Tales and Stories, with Original Engravings*, ed. Charles E. Robinson (Baltimore: Johns Hopkins Univ. Press, 1976), 33.

5. *MWSL*, 1:21—24, 180.

6. *PBSL*, 2:256—57, 292, 376.

7. *MWSL*, 1:22.

8. *MWSL*, 1:149.

9. *MWSL*, 3:369.

10. *MWSL*, 1:79—80.

11. *MWSL*, 1:101.

12. *MWSL*, 1:23.

13. *MWSL*, 1:108; *MWSJ*, 1:293.

14. See Mary Shelley, *Relation of the Death of the Family of the Cenci*, ed. Betty T. Bennett, in *The Bodleian Shelley Manuscripts*, vol. 10 (New York: Garland, 1992).

15. Mary Shelley spelled her title character's name "Mathilda" in her rough draft and fair copy but referred to the work itself as "Matilda." This discussion conforms to her usage.

16. Mary Shelley, *Relation of the Death of the Family of the Cenci*, 163.

17. For a discussion of the Romantics and incest, see Peter L. Thorslev Jr., "Incest as Romantic Symbol," *Comparative Literature Studies* 2 (1965): 56.

18. E.g., *Manfred, The Bride of Abydos*, and *Parisina*.

19. *MWSJ*, 1:226; *PBSL*, 2:39.

20. Mary Shelley, "Alfieri," in *Lives of the most Eminent Literary and Scientific Men of Italy, Spain, and Portugal, Cabinet Cyclopaedia*, 3 vols., The Cabinet of Biography, ed. Rev. Dionysius Lardner, 86–88 (London: Longman, Rees, Orme, Brown, Green, & Longman; and John Taylor, 1835–37), 2:292.

21. The review appeared in *Literary Gazette*, no. 226 (19 May 1821), and is reproduced in Donald H. Reiman, ed., *The Romantics Reviewed*, 9 vols. (New York: Garland, 1972), pt. C, vol. 2, 527–30.

22. *The British Critic* 9 (April 1818): 439.

23. *Blackwood's Edinburgh Magazine*, March 1818, 613–20; *Quarterly Review*, January 1818; *Gentleman's Magazine*, April 1818. For Mary Shelley's response to Scott's review, see *MWSL*, 1:71.

24. *S&C*, 6:161–63.

25. *MWSJ*, 2:442; see also *N&SW*, vol. 2, introductory note.

26. The following discussion draws on my essay "The Political

Philosophy of Mary Shelley's Historical Novels: *Valperga* and *Perkin Warbeck*," in *The Evidence of the Imagination*, ed. Donald H. Reiman, Michael C. Jaye, and Betty T. Bennett (New York: New York Univ. Press, 1978).

27. *Literary Gazette*, no. 319 (1 March 1823): 132–33.

28. Lodovico Antonio Muratori, *Dissertazioni sopra le Antichità Italiane* (1751), ed. Gaetano Cenni, 3 vols. (Monaco: Agostino Olzah, 1765–66), 3:255–58.

29. See *Dictionnaire de Théologie Catholique*, ed. F. Vernet, 15 vols. (Paris: Litouzey et Ane, 1954), 6, pt. 2:1981–82; *Encyclopedia of Religion and Ethics*, ed. James Hastings, 13 vols. (New York: C. Scribner's Sons, 1925–35), 5:318; and *New Catholic Encyclopedia* (Washington, D.C.: Catholic University, 1967), 14:448.

30. In her preface to the *Posthumous Poems of Percy Bysshe Shelley* she writes: "The ungrateful world did not feel his loss, and the gap it made seemed to close as quickly over his memory as the murderous sea above his living frame" (*N&SW*, 2:238); and in her preface to *The Poetical Works of Percy Bysshe Shelley* she writes: "He died, and the world shewed no outward sign; but his influence over mankind, though slow in growth, is fast augmenting, and in the ameliorations that have taken place in the political state of his country, we may trace in part the operation of his arduous struggles" (*N&SW*, 2:258). See also *MWSL*, 1:307, 336.

31. "I shall die and you will see the world confounded by a number of disturbances, and everything turned upside down" (*N&SW*, 3:325).

32. See Louis Green, *Castruccio Castracani: A Study on the Origins and*

Character of a Fourteenth-Century Italian Despotism (Oxford: Clarendon Press, 1986), 256.

33. The Congress of Vienna in 1815 drew up a federal pact for Switzerland that established twenty-two broadly autonomous cantons of governments that ranged from democratic to autocratic and a highly restricted central diet. In 1848 a new constitution structured Switzerland into a federal union modeled on the United States.

34. *MWSL*, 1:138.

35. *A Greek-English Lexicon*, rev. ed., ed. Henry Stuart Jones, 2 vols. (Oxford Clarendon Press, 1968). Mary Shelley was studying Greek during the period in which she wrote *Valperga*.

36. See, e.g., *S&C*, 3:397–422.

37. See also, "Mythological Dramas: *Proserpine* and *Midas*," ed. Charles E. Robinson, in *The Bodleian Shelley Manuscripts*, vol. 10.

38. See *MWSL*, 2:122, 161.

39. Written between 6 and 10 August 1820 (*MWSJ*, 1:328), the story was found in the family home in Italy by Cristina Dazzi.

40. See also White, *Shelley*, 1:391; and *MWSL*, 1:6–7.

41. *MWSL*, 1:450.

42. *MWSL*, 1:244–50.

43. *MWSL*, 1:249.

44. *MWSL*, 1:252, 261–62ff.

45. Eleven pages recounting P. B. Shelley's boyhood are in the

Bodleian Library (MS. Shelley, adds. c. 5). See also *MWSJ*,
1:444, 446–47.

46. See *The Liberal: Verse and Prose from the South,* 2 vols. (London:
John Hunt, 1822–23); *MWSL,* 1:286ff.; and *PBSL,* 2:343–44.
For a history of *The Liberal,* see William H. Marshall, *Byron, Shelley,
Hunt, and The Liberal* (Philadelphia: Univ. of Pennsylvania Press,
1960).

47. "A Tale" appeared in vol. 1 of *The Liberal* (1822), 289–325;
and "Madame D'Houtetot" and "Giovanni Villani" appeared
in vol. 2 (1823), 67–83 and 281–97. P. B. Shelley's "May-day
Night; a Poetical Translation from Goëthe's Faust" and "Song,
Written for an Indian Air" appeared in vol. 1, 121–37 and 397,
and his "Lines to a Critic" appeared in vol. 2, 187–88.

48. Ingpen, *Shelley in England,* 2:574–75; *MWSL,* 1:252, 382ff.;
MWSJ, 2:481.

CHAPTER THREE · Return to England, 1823–1837

1. *MWSL,* 1:369.

2. *MWSJ,* 2:487.

3. *MWSL,* 2:300. Editors who followed agree with that assess-
ment. See, e.g., Charles H. Taylor Jr., *The Early Collected Editions of
Shelley's Poems* (New Haven: Yale Univ. Press, 1958), ixff.; Irving
Massey, *Posthumous Poems of Shelley: Mary Shelley's Fair Copy Book*
(Montreal: McGill-Queens' Univ. Press, 1969), 8–9; and Ju-
dith Chernaik, *The Lyrics of Shelley* (Cleveland: The Press of Case
Western Reserve Univ., 1972), xiii.

4. *MWSL,* 1:397.

5. See Neil Fraistat, "Illegitimate Shelley: Radical Piracy and the Textual Edition as Cultural Performance," *PMLA* 109, no. 3 (1994): 420 n. 11.

6. See Taylor, *Early Collected Editions of Shelley's Poems,* ix; see also White, *Shelley,* 2:394–95.

7. *MWSL,* 1:384.

8. *MWSL,* 1:444.

9. For the most complete edition of Mary Shelley's short stories, see Robinson's *Mary Shelley: Collected Tales and Stories.*

10. In addition to being published in *The Liberal,* Mary Shelley's short stories identified to date were published in the *Appleton's Journal, The Athenaeum, The Court Magazine and Belle Assemblée, Heath's Book of Beauty, The Keepsake, The London Magazine, Original Compositions in Prose and Verse,* and *Yesterday and To-day* (see *Mary Shelley: Collected Tales and Stories,* 373–400).

11. *MWSL,* 2:108–9.

12. *MWSL,* 1:412. The word "dirt" was deleted by Mary Shelley.

13. The following discussion replicates in part my essay "Radical Imaginings: Mary Shelley's *The Last Man,*" in *The Wordsworth Circle* 26, no. 3 (1995): 147–52.

14. Examples of such readings appear in Fisch, Mellor, and Schor, *The Other Mary Shelley.*

15. I am indebted to Frederick Burwick for pointing out that Mary Shelley's use of plague to represent "social contagion" may have been influenced by Charles Brockden Brown's novel

Arthur Mervyn (1799), which Mary Shelley read in 1817. In 1825 she read William Dunlap's *Life of Charles Brockden Brown* (Philadelphia: J. P. Parke, 1815) (*MWSL*, 1:498); in 1826 she referred to the author admiringly as "Poor dear Brown" (*MWSL*, 3:402—4).

16. *MWSL*, 1:564.

17. Coleridge, in *Biographia Literaria*; Hazlitt, in a number of works, including his *Table Talk* essay about Rembrandt (James A. Houck kindly supplied this and eleven other examples of Hazlitt's use of "keeping"); P. B. Shelley, in *A Defence of Poetry*.

18. Mary Shelley commented, "The Bay of Baiae is beautiful but we are disappointed by the various places we visit" (*MWSJ*, 1:242); and P. B. Shelley writes only that they "passed thro the cavern of the Sybil (not Virgil's Sybil) which pierces one of the hills which circumscribe the lake" (*PBSL*, 2:61).

19. For Mary Shelley's role in an instance of actual gender shifting, see below, n. 33.

20. Mary Shelley expressed her view that no form of government, including republicanism, in itself was desirable unless its predominant goal was to benefit all its citizens; see, e.g., her dismissal of "republican principles & liberty, if Peace is not the offspring" (*MWSL*, 2:183).

21. Godwin, *Political and Philosophical Writings*, 3:50.

22. St Clair, *The Godwins*, 282, 283.

23. Earl Wasserman, *Shelley* (Baltimore: Johns Hopkins Press, 1971), 155.

24. Morton D. Paley, "*The Last Man:* Apocalypse without Millennium," in Fisch, Mellor, and Schor, *The Other Mary Shelley*, 107.

25. *MWSJ*, 2:442; Fiona Stafford, *The Last of the Race: The Growth of a Myth from Milton to Darwin* (Oxford: Clarendon Press, 1994), ch. 8.

26. *MWSJ*, 2:432.

27. *MWSL*, 1:260ff.

28. *MWSJ*, 1:476–77.

29. *MWSJ*, 2:543.

30. See, e.g., *Epipsychidion*, lines 163–69; and, most importantly, *Prometheus Unbound* for its thesis as well as for its form.

31. *MWSL*, 2:124.

32. *MWSL*, 1:568–69.

33. See Betty T. Bennett, *Mary Diana Dods: A Gentleman and a Scholar* (New York: Morrow, 1991; reprint, Baltimore: Johns Hopkins Univ. Press, 1994); and *MWSL*, 1:533–34, 2:7–8.

34. In 1831 Mary Shelley, editing Trelawny's works, recommended that he comply with the publisher's insistence that certain parts be "expunged" (*MWSL*, 2:131ff.); and in 1838 she initially complied with the publisher's request that parts of *Queen Mab* be omitted (*MWSL*, 2:301). For a discussion of changes P. B. Shelley made in the interest of dissemination, see *S&C*, 7:41–42.

35. Portions of this discussion appeared earlier in my essay "Political Philosophy of Mary Shelley's Historical Novels."

36. E.g., her explicit statement that the dates in her story are at variance with historical fact.

37. Mary Shelley drew on her journal in describing the devastation of war (cf., e.g., *MWSJ*, 1:12–13; and *Perkin Warbeck*, *N&SW*, 5:91–92 and n).

38. See *S&C*, 7:1–12.

39. Godwin, *Political Justice*, in Godwin, *Political and Philosophical Writings*, 3:7.

40. See, e.g., *MWSL*, 2:123–25.

41. For a comparison of Katherine Gordon's and Monina de Faro's perspectives, see *N&SW*, 5:290–91: "It was strange that a girl of royal birth, bred in a palace, accustomed to a queen-like sovereignty over her father's numerous vassals in the Highlands, should aim at restricting the ambitious York to mere privacy; while Monina, the humble daughter of a Moorish mariner, would have felt honour, reputation, all that is dear to man, at stake, if her friend had dreamed of renouncing his claims to the English crown."

42. *The Edinburgh Literary Journal; or Weekly Register of Criticism and Belles Lettres*, 19 June 1830, 351.

43. *MWSL*, 2:117–18.

44. *MWSL*, 2:119–20.

45. *MWSL*, 2:122. Owen (1801–77) became a U.S. politician and social reformer. He was the eldest son of Scottish socialist reformer Robert Owen (1771–1858), a friend of Godwin's.

46. *MWSL*, 2:124.

47. The model for the abduction was drawn from Richardson's *Clarissa*, but Mary Shelley may also have had in mind the abduction in Godwin's novel *Imogen* (Godwin, *Collected Novels*, 1:26).

CHAPTER FOUR · Last Journeys, 1837–1851

1. She contributed to vols. 86–88 of the former, cited in ch. 2, n. 19, above (hereafter cited as *Lives*, 1835–37); and vols. 102 and 103 of the latter, published in London by Longman, Orme, Brown, Green & Longman and John Taylor (hereafter cited as *Lives*, 1838–39).

2. *MWSL*, 2:219.

3. *MWSL*, 2:260.

4. *MWSL*, 2:255.

5. *MWSL*, 2:255.

6. Bennett, "Newly Uncovered Letters and Poems," 66.

7. *MWSL*, 2:293.

8. *Lives*, 1837–39, 2:341.

9. *MWSL*, 2:198, 221.

10. *MWSL*, 2:298–99.

11. *MWSL*, 2:300.

12. *MWSL*, 2:309–10; *MWSJ*, 2:559–61.

13. Newman Ivey White, "Literature and the Law of Libel: Shelley and the Radicals of 1840–42," *Studies in Philology* 22 (1925): 34–47.

14. See, e.g., Fraistat, "Illegitimate Shelley," 410.

15. *MWSL*, 3:85ff.

16. Parts of this discussion are indebted to my essay "Passport to Somewhere Else: Mary Shelley's World of Travel," in *Voyaging through Strange Seas,* ed. Timothy Webb (forthcoming).

17. See, e.g., her description of arriving at Venice, where "[d]eath hovered over the scene" (*N&SW,* 8:269); and reminders of P. B. Shelley from the view from Palazzo Mocenigo (8:271).

18. See, e.g., *Vindication, Works,* 5:113—14; *Political Justice, Political and Philosophical Writings,* 3:256.

19. *MWSL*, 2:334—35.

20. See *MWSL,* 3:281—82.

21. See, e.g., *MWSL,* 2:72, 3:284.

22. *MWSL*, 2:82.

23. See Sunstein, *Mary Shelley,* 388—97.

24. See, e.g., Fraistat, "Illegitimate Shelley," 410, 419 n. 6.

25. See, e.g., Mary Poovey, *The Proper Lady and the Woman Writer* (Chicago: Univ. of Chicago Press, 1984); and Anne K. Mellor, *Mary Shelley: Her Life, Her Fiction, Her Monsters* (New York: Methuen, 1988).

Selected Bibliography

PRIMARY WORKS BY MARY SHELLEY

Mounseer Nongtongpaw; or the Discoveries of John Bull in a Trip to Paris.
London: Proprietors of the Juvenile Library [M. J.
Godwin & Co.], 1808. Four editions published by
Godwin. Two editions published in the United States.
Mary Shelley contributed draft.

History of a Six Weeks' Tour through a Part of France, Switzerland, Germany, and Holland: With Letters Descriptive of a Sail round the Lake of Geneva, and of the Glaciers of Chamouni. [With Percy Bysshe
Shelley.] London: T. Hookham, Jun.; and C. & J.
Ollier, 1817.

Frankenstein; or, The Modern Prometheus. 3 vols. London: Lackington, Hughes, Harding, Mavor, & Jones, 1818.

Valperga; or, The Life and Adventures of Castruccio, Prince of Lucca. 3
vols. London: G. & W. B. Whittaker, 1823.

The Last Man. 3 vols. London: Henry Colburn, 1826.

The Fortunes of Perkin Warbeck, A Romance. 3 vols. London:
Henry Colburn & Richard Bentley, 1830.

Frankenstein; or, The Modern Prometheus. Revised with an introduction by "M.W.S." 3 vols. in 1. London: Henry Colburn & Richard Bentley; Edinburgh: Bell & Bradfute;
Dublin: Cumming, 1831.

Proserpine: A Mythological Drama, in Two Acts. In *The Winter's Wreath* for 1832, 1–20. London: Whittaker, Treacher, & Arnot [1831].

Lodore. 3 vols. London: Richard Bentley, 1835.

Lives of the most Eminent Literary and Scientific Men of Italy, Spain, and Portugal. [With James Montgomery and Sir David Brewster.] Vols. 1 and 2; vols. 86 and 87 of The Cabinet of Biography, edited by the Rev. Dionysius Lardner. London: Longman, Rees, Orme, Brown, Green & Longman; and John Taylor, 1835.

Lives of the most Eminent Literary and Scientific Men of Italy, Spain, and Portugal. Vol. 3; vol. 88 of The Cabinet of Biography, edited by the Rev. Dionysius Lardner. London: Longman, Orme, Brown, Green & Longmans; and John Taylor, 1837.

Falkner: A Novel. 3 vols. London: Saunders & Otley, 1837.

Lives of the most Eminent Literary and Scientific Men of France. Vols. 1 and 2; vols. 102 and 103 of The Cabinet of Biography, edited by the Rev. Dionysius Lardner. London: Longman, Orme, Brown, Green & Longmans; and John Taylor, 1838–39.

Rambles in Germany and Italy, in 1840, 1842, and 1843. 2 vols. London: Edward Moxon, 1844.

The Choice—A Poem on Shelley's Death. Edited by H. Buxton Forman. London: privately printed, 1876.

Midas. In *Proserpine & Midas: Two Unpublished Mythological Dramas by Mary Shelley*, 47–89. [1820]. Edited by A[ndre] Koszul. London: Humphrey Milford, 1922.

Matilda. [1819–20]. Edited by Elizabeth Nitchie. Chapel Hill: Univ. of North Carolina Press, 1959.

Mary Shelley: Collected Tales and Stories, with Original Engravings. Edited by

Charles E. Robinson. Baltimore: Johns Hopkins Univ. Press, 1976.

EDITED WORKS BY MARY SHELLEY

Posthumous Poems of Percy Bysshe Shelley. Edited by Mary W. Shelley. London: John and Henry L. Hunt, 1824.

The Poetical Works of Percy Bysshe Shelley. Edited by Mrs. Shelley. 4 vols. London: Edward Moxon, 1839.

The Poetical Works of Percy Bysshe Shelley. Edited by Mary W. Shelley. London: Edward Moxon, 1840 [1839]. One-volume edition with postscript.

Essays, Letters from Abroad, Translations and Fragments, By Percy Bysshe Shelley. Edited by Mrs. Shelley. 2 vols. London: Edward Moxon, 1840 [1839]. 2d ed. 1841.

SECONDARY WORKS

Bennett, Betty T. "Feminism and Editing Mary Wollstonecraft Shelley: The Editor and?/or? the Text." In *Palimpsest: Editorial Theory in the Humanities,* edited by George Bornstein and Ralph G. Williams, 67–96. Ann Arbor: Univ. of Michigan Press, 1993.

———. "Newly Uncovered Letters and Poems by Mary Wollstonecraft Shelley." *Keats-Shelley Journal* 46 (1997): 51–74.

———. "The Political Philosophy of Mary Shelley's Historical Novels: *Valperga* and *Perkin Warbeck.*" In *The Evidence of the Imagination,* edited by Donald H. Reiman, Michael C. Jaye, and Betty T. Bennett. New York: New York Univ. Press. 1978.

Bennett, Betty T., and William T. Little. "Seven Letters from

Prosper Mérimée to Mary Shelley." *Comparative Literature* 31 (1979): 134–53.

Brown, Ford K. *The Life of William Godwin.* London: J. M. Dent & Sons, 1926.

Cameron, Kenneth Neill. *Shelley: The Golden Years.* Cambridge: Harvard Univ. Press, 1974.

Cameron, Kenneth Neill, Donald E. Reiman, and Doucet Devin Fischer, eds. *Shelley and His Circle, 1773–1822.* 8 vols. to date. Cambridge: Harvard Univ. Press, 1961–.

Clairmont, Claire. *The Journals of Claire Clairmont.* Edited by Marion Kingston Stocking with David Mackenzie Stocking. Cambridge: Harvard Univ. Press, 1968.

Clairmont, Claire, Charles Clairmont, and Fanny Imlay Godwin. *The Clairmont Correspondence: Letters of Claire Clairmont, Charles Clairmont, and Fanny Imlay Godwin.* Edited by Marion Kingston Stocking. 2 vols. Baltimore: Johns Hopkins Univ. Press, 1995.

Dowden, Edward. *The Life of Percy Bysshe Shelley.* London: Kegan Paul, Trench & Co., 1886.

Dunbar, Clement. *A Bibliography of Shelley Studies: 1823–1950.* New York: Garland, 1976.

Fisch, Audrey A., Anne K. Mellor, and Esther H. Schor, eds. *The Other Mary Shelley: Beyond Frankenstein.* New York: Oxford Univ. Press, 1993.

Gilbert, Sandra, and Susan Gubar. *The Madwoman in the Attic.* New Haven: Yale Univ. Press, 1979.

Gisborne, Maria, and Edward E. Williams. *Maria Gisborne & Edward E. Williams, Shelley's Friends: Their Journals and Letters.* Edited by Frederick L. Jones. Norman: Univ. of Oklahoma Press, 1951.

Godwin, William. *The Collected Novels and Memoirs of William Godwin.*

Edited by Mark Philp. 8 vols. London: Pickering & Chatto, 1992.

———. *The Political and Philosophical Writings of William Godwin*. Edited by Martin Fitzpatrick with an introduction by Mark Philp. 7 vols. London: Pickering & Chatto, 1993.

Holmes, Richard. *Shelley: The Pursuit*. London: Weidenfeld & Nicolson, 1974.

Ingpen, Roger. *Shelley in England: New Facts and Letters from the Shelley-Whitton Papers*. 2 vols. Boston: Houghton Mifflin, 1917.

Ketterer, David. *Frankenstein's Creation: The Book, the Monster, and Human Reality*. English Literature Studies No. 16. Victoria, B.C.: Victoria Univ. Press, 1979.

Levine, George, and U. C. Knoepflmacher, eds. *The Endurance of Frankenstein: Essays on Mary Shelley's Novel*. Berkeley: Univ. of California Press, 1979.

Lyles, W. H. *Mary Shelley: An Annotated Bibliography*. New York: Garland, 1975.

Marchand, Leslie A. *Byron: A Biography*. 3 vols. New York: Alfred A. Knopf, 1957.

Marshall, Mrs. Julian. *The Life and Letters of Mary Wollstonecraft Shelley*. 2 vols. London: Richard Bentley & Sons, 1889.

Mellor, Anne K. *Mary Shelley: Her Life, Her Fiction, Her Monsters*. London: Methuen, 1988.

Murray, E. B. "Shelley's Contribution to Mary's *Frankenstein*." *Keats-Shelley Memorial Bulletin* 29 (1978): 50–68.

Nitchie, Elizabeth. *Mary Shelley: "Author of Frankenstein."* New Brunswick: Rutgers Univ. Press, 1953.

Norman, Sylva. *Flight of the Skylark: The Development of Shelley's Reputation*. London: Max Reinhardt, 1954.

Palacio, Jean de. *Mary Shelley dans son oeuvre: Contributions aux etudes shelleyennes.* Paris: Editions Klincksieck, 1969.

Paul, C. Kegan. *William Godwin: His Friends and Contemporaries.* 2 vols. London: Henry S. King & Co., 1876.

Polidori, John. *The Diary of Dr. John William Polidori.* Edited by William Michael Rossetti. London: Elkin Mathews, 1911.

Rolleston, Maud. *Talks with Lady Shelley.* London: George G. Harrap & Co., 1925.

Sanborn, F. B., ed. *The Romance of Mary W. Shelley, John Howard Payne, and Washington Irving.* Boston: Boston Bibliophile Society, 1907.

Shelley, Jane, Lady, ed. *Shelley and Mary.* 4 vols. London: privately printed, 1882.

Shelley, Mary. *The Frankenstein Notebooks.* Edited by Charles E. Robinson. 2 vols. The Manuscripts of the Younger Romantics, edited by Donald H. Reiman, 9. New York: Garland, 1996.

———. *The Journals of Mary Shelley, 1814–1844.* Edited by Paula R. Feldman and Diana Scott-Kilvert. 2 vols. Oxford: Clarendon Press, 1987. Reprint. Baltimore: Johns Hopkins Univ. Press, 1995.

———. *The Letters of Mary Wollstonecraft Shelley.* Edited by Betty T. Bennett. 3 vols. Baltimore: Johns Hopkins Univ. Press, 1980–88.

———. "Mythological Dramas: *Proserpine* and *Midas.*" Edited by Charles E. Robinson. In *The Bodleian Shelley Manuscripts,* vol. 10. New York: Garland, 1992.

———. *The Novels and Selected Works of Mary Shelley.* Gen. ed. Nora

Crook with Pamela Clemit; consulting ed. Betty T. Bennett. 8 vols. London: William Pickering, 1996.

———. *Relation of the Death of the Family of the Cenci.* Edited by Betty T. Bennett. In *The Bodleian Shelley Manuscripts,* vol. 10. New York: Garland, 1992.

Shelley, Percy Bysshe. *The Complete Works of Percy Bysshe Shelley.* Edited by Roger Ingpen and Walter E. Peck. Julian Edition. 10 vols. London: E. Benn, 1926–30.

———. *The Letters of Percy Bysshe Shelley.* Edited by Frederick L. Jones. 2 vols. Oxford: Clarendon Press, 1964.

Small, Christopher. *Ariel Like a Harpy; Shelley, Mary and Frankenstein.* London: Victor Gollancz, 1972.

Spacks, Patricia Meyer. *The Female Imagination.* New York: Avon Books, 1975.

Spark, Muriel. *Child of Light: A Reassessment of Mary Shelley.* Hadleigh, Essex: Tower Bridge Publications, 1951. Revised as *Mary Shelley* (New York: E. P. Dutton, 1987).

St Clair, William. *The Godwins and the Shelleys: The Biography of a Family.* Boston and London: Faber & Faber, 1989. Reprint. Baltimore: Johns Hopkins Univ. Press, 1991.

Sunstein, Emily W. *Mary Shelley: Romance and Reality.* Boston: Little, Brown, 1989. Reprint. Baltimore: Johns Hopkins Univ. Press, 1991.

Veeder, William. *Mary Shelley and Frankenstein: The Fate of Androgyny.* Chicago: Univ. of Chicago Press, 1986.

Walling, William A. *Mary Shelley.* New York: Twayne, 1972.

White, Newman Ivey. *Shelley.* 2 vols. Rev. ed. London: Secker & Warburg, 1947.

Wollstonecraft, Mary. *The Works of Mary Wollstonecraft.* Edited by
Marilyn Butler and Janet Todd. 7 vols. London: Pickering &
Chatto, 1989.

———. *A Short Residence in Sweden, Norway and Denmark,* and William
Godwin, *Memoirs of the Author of The Rights of Woman.* Edited with
an introduction and notes by Richard Holmes. London:
Penguin, 1987.

Index

education: William Godwin's
views on, 8, 13–14; Mary
Shelley's views on, 1; Mary
Wollstonecraft's views on, 13
"English in Italy, The" (review;
Mary Shelley), 70–71
Epipsychidion (P. B. Shelley), 63
Esdaile, Ianthe Shelley. *See*
Shelley, Ianthe
*Essays, Letters from Abroad, Transla-
tions and Fragments by Percy Bysshe
Shelley* (Mary W. Shelley,
ed.), 110

Falkner: A Novel (Mary Shelley),
97–104; reviews of, 102–3;
as sociopolitical commen-
tary, 101–2
*"1572 Chronique du Temps de Charles
IX"* (review; Mary Shelley),
71
"Fire, Famine, and Slaughter:
A War Eclogue" (Coleridge),
88
*Fortunes of Perkin Warbeck, The; A Ro-
mance* (Mary Shelley). See
Perkin Warbeck
France, as viewed by Mary
Shelley, 27–28
*Frankenstein; or, the Modern
Prometheus* (Mary Shelley), 2,
23, 64, 80, 85; interpretations of, 30–37, 38–42; re-

views of, 52; introduction
to, 10–11, 17

Galloni, Laura (Tighe), 119
Galvani, Luigi, 39
Ghibellines, civil war with
Guelphs, 54–61
Gibson, Thomas, 119
Gilbert, William, 38
"Giovanni Villani" (Mary Shel-
ley), 64, 70, 75
Gisborne, John, 43
Gisborne, Maria, 43
Godwin, Fanny Imlay, 8, 9, 15,
145n.32; death of, 21
Godwin, Mary Jane Clairmont,
80, 147n.45; marriage to
William Godwin, 8–9; rela-
tionship with Mary Shelley,
14–15
Godwin, Mary Wollstonecraft.
See Wollstonecraft, Mary
Godwin, William, 145n.32,
150n.85; children's books
by, 14; as editor of works of
Mary Wollstonecraft, 11–12;
estrangement from Mary
Shelley, 18–19, 20; family
life of, 8–10; as influence on
Mary Shelley, 1–2; political
views of, 1–2, 4–5, 17–18.
Works: *Bible Stories* [pseud.
William Scolfield], 14; *Caleb*

Library of Congress Cataloging-in-Publication Data

Bennett, Betty T.

Mary Wollstonecraft Shelley : an introduction /
Betty T. Bennett.

  p.   cm.

Includes bibliographical references and index.

ISBN 0-8018-5975-1 (alk. paper). —

ISBN 0-8018-5976-x (pbk.: alk. paper)

1. Shelley, Mary Wollstonecraft, 1797–1851—Criticism and interpretation. 2. Literature and society—England—History—19th century. 3. Women and literature—England—History—19th century. 4. Social problems in literature. I. Title.

PR5398.B46   1998   98-16237

823'.7—dc21   CIP